SUCCESSFUL MARRIAGE

ARVIND UPADHYAY

Marriages take work, commitment, and love, but they also need respect to be truly happy and successful. A marriage based on love and respect doesn't just happen. Both spouses have to do their part.

The purpose of this book is to find out "What makes a Successful Marriage". It seeks to examine what the important ingredients are that will contribute to marital satisfaction. This research utilises the strength approach in finding out what works in a marriage. Once we know what they are, we can in turn, propagate and teach couples these important marital strengths to help them build happy and successful marriages. The target respondents of this research are couples who have been married for five years and above. The reason is because the Singapore law requires that a couple to be separated for at least 3 years before they can proceed to file for divorce. It is important to exclude the latter group so that we study marriages that are still intact. The methodology adopted is quantitative in nature, i.e. using a survey questionnaire that was administered via the internet with the invaluable assistance of NTUC Income whose data base has over 1.8 million policy holders in Singapore. The sample size of 3,000 yielded a total of 310 respondents which is a relatively good return rate of 10.3%, based on existing norm for internet surveys. To gain a better understanding of the research subject and to help me conceptualise and design the questionnaire, 3 focus group discussions were conducted. One was with service providers or professionals working with couples in counseling and/or premarital/marriage education setting. The other 2 focus groups were conducted with a group
of married couples.
Dr Olson's Enrich Marital Satisfaction Scale (EMS) was used in the questionnaire. It
showed a high reliability in my sample with an overall Alpha value of 0.889. In Dr Olson's
EMS, there is an implicit assumption that the ten item variables are able to explain marital
satisfaction equally. In an attempt to fine tune and build on Dr Olson's method for measuring
marital satisfaction, I developed a weighted EMS Score for Singapore

marriages.
Results showed that there were substantial differences in the importance of the 10
variables as determined by the t-tests, which ranged from 3.71 for satisfaction with common
leisure activities to 0.68 for agreement on financial decisions. From an empirical perspective,
results revealed that conducting regressions using the weighted EMS produced slightly higher
adjusted R squares and t values than using the un-weighted EMS as a dependent variable.
Using stepwise multiple regressions, a model of marital strength factors was
developed to explain and predict marital satisfaction using weighted EMS. The result was the
identification of 6 factors that could explain and predict marital satisfaction. Next, I
developed a conceptual illustration of these 6 Marriage Pillars© for practitioners, marriage
educators and policy makers when working with couples to build happy and successful
marriages. Successful marriages are the pillars of a strong society. These 6 Marriage Pillars©
were identified as Communication, Consensus, Conflict Styles, Common Leisure, Sexual
Contentment and Confiding in Spouse. This model was further refined when gender was taken into account. It was found that
only 5 pillars were significant for male and female. Both shared the same first 4 marriage
pillars but the 5th pillar was different. The 5th pillar for the males was Confide in Spouse and
Sexual Contentment for the females respectively. The order of importance was also slightly
different for males and females except for the first 2 pillars. Hence, the 5 Marriage Pillars©
for males were Communication, Consensus, Common Leisure, Conflict

Styles and Confide in
Spouse. The 5 Marriage Pillars© for females were Communication,
Consensus, Conflict
Styles, Sexual Contentment and Common Leisure.

Contents

1

Rationale for Research on Marriage

What is different about couples who stay married? What are the secrets of these
couples who manage to stay married and happy?
This study seeks to understand and examine the critical factors that contribute to
marital satisfaction. To do so, we need to study the marriages of couples who are still
married.
There is a dearth of research in the area of marriage in Singapore. There are many
research studies on divorce and the reasons why couples divorce, using the pathology or
problem approach. However, not many studies tell us why a marriage stays intact.
A review of local research yielded only 2 studies on marriage and marital
satisfaction – a Masters thesis on marital satisfaction of dual earner couples (Kwan, 1992)
and a Honours thesis on spousal roles and marital satisfaction (Lee, 2001). Both studies
were similar in the sense that they studied the effects of marital roles on marital satisfaction.
Wallerstein (1995), an authority on the study of divorce,

concluded that research on
happy marriages was in its infancy when she was embarking on her qualitative study of
"The Good Marriage". She commented that we know a great deal about marriages that fail,
for many couples seek counseling when their relationships are unable to weather the
inevitable crises of life. But while studies of marital problems and divorce now overflow
many library shelves, the entire body of research on happy marriages would fill less than half a shelf. It has always been easier to identify the dark forces that spell misery than to understand what contributes to happiness.
This research draws upon the "Strength Perspective" (Weick, Rapp, Sullivan and
Kisthardt, 1989; Miley, K.K., O'Melia, M., DuBois, B. 1998). It would be useful for us to
know why couples in Singapore decide and make the commitment to remain married.
Learning from these couples will help us to understand the critical issues that are important
to a marriage. The findings would provide insights for married couples to protect and keep
their marriage intact. It would also help social workers and counselors to know the concrete
areas to focus on when they help couples in therapy to get their marriage back on track.
Only when we know what works in a marriage, will we be able to propagate and teach
couples these values and behaviours, so that they will also be able to enjoy a successful and
happy marriage. Perhaps of more value in terms of practice, this research will affirm or
inform marriage educators on the content of their work with couples either in terms of premarital education or marital enrichment work.
1.2 Marriage Trends in Singapore
According to the Singapore Statistics Department (2005),

over a ten year period, the

mean age at first marriage for males has increased from 29.4 in 1995 to 30.5 in 2004.

Likewise, the mean age at first marriage for females has increased from 26.4 in 1995 to 27.3

in 2004. The total marriages registered under the Women's Charter and the Muslim Law

Act decreased substantially by 8.2%, from 24,519 in 1995 to 22,505 in 2004. The marriage

rate fell 24.3% from 56.3 to 42.6 per 1,000 unmarried residents in 2004 compared to 10

years ago. Likewise, the divorce rate per 1,000 married residents rose 21% to 7.5 in 2004 compared to 10 years ago (see Table 1 below). Table 1: Trends in number of marriages and divorces over a 10 year period 1995 2004 Total number of resident marriages (Women's Charter & Muslim Law Act) 24,519 22,505 Marriage rate (per '000 unmarried residents) 56.3 42.6 Total number of divorces and annulments 4,298 6,388 Divorce rate (per '000 married residents) 6.2 7.5 Source: Family Matters, Report of the Public Education Committee on Family January 2002, MCDS. and Singapore Statistics Dept, Population Trends 2005. According to the Statistics on Marriages and Divorces (2000), the number of annulments under the Women's Charter peaked at 606 in 1991. Thereafter, it dropped to an all-time low of 140 in 1993 and gradually increased to 262 in 1998 before falling to 217 in 2000 and then rising to 341 in 2004. The decline could be attributed to stricter rules being applied by the Supreme Court in granting annulments to "marriage not consummated". The total number of divorces and annulments in 1995 was 4,298 and it rose 48.6% to 6,388 in 2004. The mean of the duration of marriage for annulment was 2.4 years in 2000. The mean duration of marriages for divorces was 12.9 years in 2004 (Singapore Statistics Department, 2005). The pattern of annulments in Singapore corresponds somewhat to the western statistics and observation that the initial 3 years of the marriage are the most vulnerable years (National Centre for Health Statistics, 1995). Current statistics in the United States of America shows that most divorces occur for couples married less than five years and that the proportion of divorces is highest for couples married three years. (National Centre for Health Statistics, 1995). From the above, it is clear that the institution of marriage may be at risk and we can therefore understand the Singapore government's urgent efforts to increase the rate of marriages and encourage couples to have more babies. I would like to propose that the government, service providers and marriage champions to also pay attention to the "micro" aspects of a marriage. It is just as important to help marriages sustain longevity and if possible, to go one step further – i.e. find out what creates a happy and lasting marriage and then to propagate and teach couples to build happy and successful marriages, which is the objective of this research. Having babies may be important for population replacement, but raising babies within an environment of happy and successful marriages will ensure that our next generation will grow up to be positive and psychologically healthy people who will contribute to the society's overall well being.

1.3 Focus of Research The primary goal of this study is to understand and identify contributing factors (which I will call "marital strength factors") that are responsible for successful marriages, defined here as marital satisfaction. A second goal is to identify the relative importance of each of these factors. Marital satisfaction is the subjective satisfaction with the marital situation as a whole. It is not the purpose of this research to study satisfaction in specific areas, for >

5

2

LITERATURE REVIEW

Current literature and research studies show that certain factors are important to the stability of marriage and some of these factors will be elaborated in the paragraphs that follow. 2.1 Etiological Factors Peck and Manocherian (1989) summarised in their Chapter – Divorce in the Changing Family Life Cycle, the following etiological factors associated with marital instability: a) Age and premarital pregnancy Brides less than 18, husbands less than 20 (Norton and Glick, 1976), or couples who marry when there was a premarital pregnancy (Furstenberg, 1976) were twice as likely to divorce. b) Education Less educated men and better educated women were more at risk than better educated men and less educated women (Levinger, 1976). Compared with those who did not complete college or, have postgraduate degrees, women who have had completed four years of college was the group least at risk for divorce (Glick, 1984). c) Income Women who earned more money were more likely to divorce than women with lower incomes (Ross and Sawhill, 1975). The greater the wife's income in relation to the husband's income, the greater the risk of divorce (Cherlin, 1979).d) Employment
When the husband had unstable employment and income, or his income declined
from the previous year, the marriage was at higher risk (Ross and Sawhill, 1975).
e) Socioeconomic level

Though the gap was narrowing, the relatively disadvantaged tended to be
disproportionately at risk (Norton and Glick, 1976).
f) Race
Black couples had a higher divorce rate than whites and inter-racial marriages were
even more at risk (Norton and Glick, 1976).
g) Intergenerational transmission link
Divorce appears to run in families, though studies on the correlation between
parental divorce and marital instability in the next generation have yielded mixed
results. One possibility is that it was not the pattern of divorce per se but economic
factors related to the divorce that often push children into early marriages with
poorly selected mates (Mueller and Pope, 1977).

2.2 Marital Interaction Processes
Gottman, et al (1998) in his study of 130 newlywed couples in a laboratory setting
found that it was the marital interaction processes that were predictive of divorce or marital
stability. He also studied the processes that discriminate between happily and unhappily
married stable couples. He found that no support was found for models of anger as a
dangerous emotion, active listening or negative affect reciprocity. The pattern of
communication in couples was very important to predict marital happiness. In two
longitudinal studies, Gottman (1994) found that it was not anger that led to unhappy
marriages which in turn predicted divorce, but rather the

four processes that he called the "four Horsemen of the Apocalypse", i.e. criticism, defensiveness, contempt and stonewalling (or listener withdrawal). Gottman advocated an interaction pattern where wives should raise issues more gently and husbands should be more readily acceptable to their wives' influence. What seems significant for predicting divorce is the husband's rejection of his wife's influence, negative start-up by the wife, a lack of de-escalation of low intensity negative wife affect by the husband, or a lack of de-escalation of high intensity husband negative affect by the wife, and a lack of physiological soothing of the male.

2.3 Effects of Family of Origin

How we feel towards our intimate partner was found to be determined partly by the

relationships we experienced in our family of origin. It has been well documented that

current relationship problems often were simply repeated patterns from past relationships.

Williamson (1981) found that the way individuals resolved family of origin relationship

issues determined how they handled similar matters in all of their relationships. Most

research suggested that individuals who experienced poor relationships with their parents

were more likely to have adjustment difficulties in their intimate relationships (Schnarch

1991, 1997; Wallerstein and Blakeslee, 1995) and that poor marital and parent-child

relationships predicted lower quality and stability in the offspring's long-term intimate

relationships (Rodgers, 1996).

Attitudes toward marriage and divorce were also affected by one's family

background (Wallerstein, 2000). Some people brought up in very unhappy homes

developed negative attitudes toward marriage. Their parents'

marriage was not a good
model for marital success. What about people whose parents were divorced? Children of
divorced parents have goals for and attitudes toward marriage and family that were similar
to those children from intact families. They want long-term, loving, rewarding relationships
with their spouses (Wallerstein, 2000). However, adult children of divorced parents
expressed more accepting attitudes toward divorce than people who grew up with both
biological parents, unless their family was conflictive (Amato and Booth, 1991).

2.4 Effects of Parental Divorce
In the United States, first marriages have a 45% chance of breaking up and second
marriages have a 60% chance ending up in divorce. In her longitudinal study of 25 years,
Wallerstein (2000) studied the lives of 131 children whose parents were going through
divorce. Using a comparison group of adults who grew up in the same communities,
Wallerstein showed how adult children of divorce essentially viewed life differently from
their peers raised in intact homes where parents also confronted marital difficulties but
decided on balance to stay together. This report challenged the myths and our fundamental
beliefs about divorce.
From the viewpoint of the children, and countered to what happened to their parents,
divorce was a cumulative experience. Its impact increased over time and rise to a crescendo
in adulthood (Wallerstein, 2000).

When children of divorce reached adulthood, it affected their search for love, sexual intimacy and commitment. The lack of good model left them unprepared for adult relationships. Many ended up with unsuitable or very troubled partners. In contrast, adults from reasonable good or even moderately unhappy families understood the demands and sacrifices required in close relationships, having watched their parents, struggle, cope and overcome their difficulties in marriage (Wallerstein, 2000 pp. 300). Wallerstein (2000) called for efforts to strengthen marriages and the need to appreciate the difficulties modern couples faced in balancing work and family. She concluded that it was no accident that 80% of divorces occurred in the first nine years of a marriage (Wallerstein, 2000 pp. 303)

Wallerstein (2000) called for efforts to strengthen marriages and the need to
appreciate the difficulties modern couples faced in balancing work and family. She
concluded that it was no accident that 80% of divorces occurred in the first nine years of a
marriage (Wallerstein, 2000 pp. 303)

2.5 Criteria for Evaluating Marital Success
What constitutes a successful marriage? DeGenova and Rice (2002) suggested that
the four criteria for successful marriage were durability, approximation of ideals, fulfillment
of needs and satisfaction.

The definition of durability was that a marriage that last was more successful than

one that ended up in divorce. In many cases, marital stability and marital quality went hand

in hand. However, there were some marriages that lasted a lifetime but were filled with

hatred, conflict and frustration and which did not end up in divorce.

Approximation of ideals referred to the extent the couple's expectation or ideals

were fulfilled in the marriage. Another criterion of marital success was whether the

marriage fulfilled the individual's needs including psychological, social, sexual and material

needs.

2.6 Twelve characteristics of successful marriages

In their review of numerous research studies, DeGenova and Rice (2002) delineated

12 characteristics of successful marriages. These were:

(1) Communication

Good communication was one of the most important requirements in a

successful marriage. However, not all communication was helpful.

Communication could either be productive or destructive to a relationship.

Saying critical, hurtful things in a cold, unfeeling way may worsen a

relationship. Thus, politeness, tact and consideration were needed if

communication was to be productive.

(2) Admiration and respect

The most successful marriages were those in which acceptance and appreciation were partly fulfilled in the relationship (Cousins and Vincent

1983). Spouses, who showed appreciation and admired each other's

achievements and supported each other in their endeavors, were fulfilling

their emotional needs and building their self-esteem. Respect in marriage

encompassed respect for individual differences and respect for the other

person as an important human being.

Page 13

(3) Companionship
One important reason for getting married was companionship. Successful
married couples spent sufficient time together – they have interests and
friends in common.
(4) Spirituality and Values
Successful couples shared similar beliefs and values, goals and philosophy of
life. Filsinger and Wilson (1983) conducted a study of marital adjustment of
208 married couples and found that religiosity (measured in terms of
religious belief, ritual, experience, knowledge and the social consequences of
religion) was the most consistent and strongest predictor of marital
adjustment. This was in agreement with other studies that show religiosity to
be correlated to marital adjustment, marital satisfaction (Bell, Daly and
Gonzalez, 1987), with marital success (Curran, 1983; Stinnett and DeFrain,

1985) and with marital stability (Glenn and Supancic, 1984; Lauer and
Lauer, 1985).
(5) Commitment
Successful marriage required a high degree of motivation: the desire to make
the marriage work and a willingness to expend time and effort to make sure
it did. Commitment here encompassed the commitment to the self (the desire
to grow, to change and to be a good marriage partner), the commitment to
each other and the commitment to the relationship, the marriage and the
family.
Page 14

(6) Affection
One important expectation of marriage was that couples will meet each
other's need for love and affection. Affection could be both verbal and
physical. It was important for couples to agree on how to show affection and
how often.
(7) The ability to deal with crises and stress
Successful married couples were able to solve their problems and managed
stress in a creative manner. They developed problem solving skills so they
can cope (Curran, 1983). They also have a higher tolerance for frustration
and are more emotionally mature and stable. They have learned healthy,
constructive ways of dealing with anger, rather than taking it out on other
family members (Hardy, Orzek and Heistad, 1984).

(8) Responsibility
A successful marriage depends on mutual assumption, sharing and division
of responsibility in the family. Two conditions were found to be important.
First, the partners must feel that there was a fairly equal division of labour
(in household chores, childcare responsibilities etc). Second, the gender role
performances must match gender role expectations.
Page 15

(9) Unselfishness
The most successful marriages were based on a spirit of mutual helpfulness,
with each partner unselfishly attending to the needs of the other as well as to
his or her own (Bell, Daly and Gonzalez, 1987).
(10) Empathy and sensitivity
Empathy or the ability to identify with the feelings, thoughts and attitudes of
another person was an important ingredient in a successful marriage.
(11) Honesty, trust and fidelity
In successful marriages, partners know that they could accept each other's
word, believed in each other, and depended on each other to keep promises
and to be faithful to commitments made.
(12) Adaptability, flexibility and tolerance
Adaptability and flexibility required a high degree of emotional maturity.
People have to be secured enough to let go of the old thoughts and habits that
were no longer functional or appropriate. But to let go requires some
confidence that the new will work as the old. Flexible people

are not

threatened by change. Instead, they welcomed change as an opportunity to

grow.

Page 16

2.7 Other studies on marriages

2.7.1 Situational Factors

Arlene Skolnick (1981) examined marriages selected from a large longitudinal study

of adult lives. Comparing data from two interviews ten years apart, without any

observations about the couple's interactions, she concluded that marital relationships have a

high potential for change and do not necessarily decline over the years. She proposed that

situational factors such as money, health, and career success were of major importance in

marital contentment or unhappiness.

2.7.2 Friendship, commitment and shared values

Two recent studies of long-lasting marriages, by Lauer and Lauer (1987) and

Kaslow and Hammerschmidt (1992) were based largely on data from mailed questionnaires.

Both studies reported the importance of friendship, commitment and shared values, and

both found many long lasting marriages that were unhappy.

2.7.3 Cohabitation and its effects on eventual marriage

A common reason for cohabitation was for couples to assess if they were compatible

as marriage partners. However, research findings showed that cohabitation was often related

to lower marital satisfaction (Booth and Johnson, 1998).

Lichter et al (1999) found that cohabitation with one's eventual spouse produced

little difference in the marital satisfaction of women. For men, regardless of their previous

Page 17

marital history, those who did not cohabit were significantly more likely to report being
very happy than those who had.

Teachman and DeMaris (2003) found that women who had premarital sex and
cohabited only with their future husband did not affect their future chance of divorce. They
also found that having multiple premarital sex partners enhanced women's risk of divorce,
regardless of their cohabitation experiences.
2.7.3 Common Leisure and Marital Satisfaction
Crawford (2002) in a longitudinal study of 73 couples over a period of more than 13
years found that engagement in leisure activities (whether as a couple or by the husband
alone) that the husband liked but not the wife, was both a cause and a consequence of the
wives' dissatisfaction. However, when couples engaged in leisure that both liked, it resulted
in the husband being happier than the wife.
2.7.4 Relationship Skills and Compatible Personalities
McNulty and Karney (2004) studied 82 couples in a four-year marriage study within
a few months of marriage. They found that couples were happier in their marriages if they
had a true view of their relationship and the skills to work through problems. Husbands and
wives with poor relationship skills and high hopes for happiness experienced deep declines
in satisfaction.
The University of Iowa's Marital Assessment Project found that shared moral values
were less important than compatible personalities for a good

marriage (Klohnen, 2005).
Page 18

These married couples shared the same attitudes about faith and other values, but those with
same personalities were the happiest. Personality similarity accounted for 40 percent to 50
percent of marital satisfaction.
2.7.5 Companionship Marriage Model
In Hong Kong, it was found that there has been a shift of the traditional goal for
marriage from reproduction and survival of the family to that of attaining personal
satisfaction, mutual support from each other and companionship (Yeung and Kwong, 1998).
Couples that had strong beliefs about the importance of marriage had a higher chance of
withstanding marital crisis. Hence, couples who have high commitment to their marriage
would not abandon their marriage when faced with a crisis (Leung et al, 2005).
2.7.6 Roles and expectations
Two studies in Singapore studied the effects of role relationships on marital
satisfaction. Lee (2001) reported in her quantitative study of 60 Chinese couples that there
was a general trend towards egalitarian role sharing in a marriage and that role conflict and
role competence were better predictors of marital satisfaction. Kwan (1992) found that the
first predictor of marital satisfaction was the relative deprivation in the marital situation,
especially for that of the wives. This was a negative relationship, i.e. the more unfavourable
a person perceives her marriage when compared with friends or relative, the lower the
marital satisfaction. The second predictor was consensus on

marital role expectations and
the third best predictor was the quality of the spouse's role enactment.
Page 19

2.8 Top Ten Strengths of Happy Marriages (Enrich)
Based on a national study of 21,501 married couples from all 50 states and using a
comprehensive marital assessment tool called ENRICH which focused on 20 significant
areas and 195 questions, David Olson (2000) found that happy and unhappy couples
differed in five key areas and ranked them in order of importance: (1) how well partners
communicate, (2) how flexible they were as a couple, (3) how emotionally close they were,
(4) how compatible their personalities were and (5) how they handled conflict.
Olson also identified five other areas that affected a couple's happiness: (1) the
sexual relationship, (2) the choice of leisure activities, (3) the influence of family and
friends, (4) the ability to manage finances and (5) agreement on spiritual beliefs.
Olson's encouraged couples and professionals to focus on strengths of the marriage
rather than on only problems. He advised that, in order to build strength as a couple,
partners should pay the same sort of attention to the relationship that they did when they
were dating and to praise the other partner for the positive attributes, instead of focusing on
what bothers them about the partner.

marriage fulfilled the individual's needs including psychological, social, sexual and material
needs.
2.6 Twelve characteristics of successful marriages
In their review of numerous research studies, DeGenova and Rice (2002) delineated
12 characteristics of successful marriages. These were:
(1) Communication
Good communication was one of the most important requirements in a
successful marriage. However, not all communication was helpful.
Communication could either be productive or destructive to a relationship.
Saying critical, hurtful things in a cold, unfeeling way may worsen a
relationship. Thus, politeness, tact and consideration were needed if
communication was to be productive.
(2) Admiration and respect
The most successful marriages were those in which acceptance and
appreciation were partly fulfilled in the relationship (Cousins and Vincent
1983). Spouses, who showed appreciation and admired each other's
achievements and supported each other in their endeavors, were fulfilling
their emotional needs and building their self-esteem. Respect in marriage
encompassed respect for individual differences and respect for the other
person as an important human being.

Page 13

(3) Companionship
One important reason for getting married was companionship. Successful
married couples spent sufficient time together – they have interests and
friends in common.
(4) Spirituality and Values
Successful couples shared similar beliefs and values, goals and philosophy of
life. Filsinger and Wilson (1983) conducted a study of marital adjustment of
208 married couples and found that religiosity (measured in terms of
religious belief, ritual, experience, knowledge and the social consequences of
religion) was the most consistent and strongest predictor of marital
adjustment. This was in agreement with other studies that show religiosity to
be correlated to marital adjustment, marital satisfaction (Bell, Daly and
Gonzalez, 1987), with marital success (Curran, 1983; Stinnett and DeFrain,
1985) and with marital stability (Glenn and Supancic, 1984; Lauer and
Lauer, 1985).
(5) Commitment
Successful marriage required a high degree of motivation: the desire to make
the marriage work and a willingness to expend time and effort to make sure
it did. Commitment here encompassed the commitment to the self (the desire
to grow, to change and to be a good marriage partner), the commitment to
each other and the commitment to the relationship, the marriage and the
family.

Page 14

(6) Affection
One important expectation of marriage was that couples will meet each
other's need for love and affection. Affection could be both verbal and
physical. It was important for couples to agree on how to show affection and
how often.
(7) The ability to deal with crises and stress
Successful married couples were able to solve their problems and managed
stress in a creative manner. They developed problem solving skills so they
can cope (Curran, 1983). They also have a higher tolerance for frustration
and are more emotionally mature and stable. They have learned healthy,
constructive ways of dealing with anger, rather than taking it out on other
family members (Hardy, Orzek and Heistad, 1984).
(8) Responsibility
A successful marriage depends on mutual assumption, sharing and division
of responsibility in the family. Two conditions were found to be important.
First, the partners must feel that there was a fairly equal division of labour
(in household chores, childcare responsibilities etc). Second, the gender role
performances must match gender role expectations.
Page 15

(9) Unselfishness
The most successful marriages were based on a spirit of

mutual helpfulness,
with each partner unselfishly attending to the needs of the other as well as to
his or her own (Bell, Daly and Gonzalez, 1987).
(10) Empathy and sensitivity
Empathy or the ability to identify with the feelings, thoughts and attitudes of
another person was an important ingredient in a successful marriage.
(11) Honesty, trust and fidelity
In successful marriages, partners know that they could accept each other's
word, believed in each other, and depended on each other to keep promises
and to be faithful to commitments made.
(12) Adaptability, flexibility and tolerance
Adaptability and flexibility required a high degree of emotional maturity.
People have to be secured enough to let go of the old thoughts and habits that
were no longer functional or appropriate. But to let go requires some
confidence that the new will work as the old. Flexible people are not
threatened by change. Instead, they welcomed change as an opportunity to
grow.
Page 16

2.7 Other studies on marriages
2.7.1 Situational Factors
Arlene Skolnick (1981) examined marriages selected from a large longitudinal study
of adult lives. Comparing data from two interviews ten years apart, without any
observations about the couple's interactions, she concluded that marital relationships have a

high potential for change and do not necessarily decline over the years. She proposed that
situational factors such as money, health, and career success were of major importance in
marital contentment or unhappiness.
2.7.2 Friendship, commitment and shared values
Two recent studies of long-lasting marriages, by Lauer and Lauer (1987) and
Kaslow and Hammerschmidt (1992) were based largely on data from mailed questionnaires.
Both studies reported the importance of friendship, commitment and shared values, and
both found many long lasting marriages that were unhappy.
2.7.3 Cohabitation and its effects on eventual marriage
A common reason for cohabitation was for couples to assess if they were compatible
as marriage partners. However, research findings showed that cohabitation was often related
to lower marital satisfaction (Booth and Johnson, 1998).
Lichter et al (1999) found that cohabitation with one's eventual spouse produced
little difference in the marital satisfaction of women. For men, regardless of their previous
Page 17

marital history, those who did not cohabit were significantly more likely to report being
very happy than those who had.

Teachman and DeMaris (2003) found that women who had premarital sex and
cohabited only with their future husband did not affect their future chance of divorce. They
also found that having multiple premarital sex partners enhanced women's risk of divorce,
regardless of their cohabitation experiences.

2.7.3 Common Leisure and Marital Satisfaction
Crawford (2002) in a longitudinal study of 73 couples over a period of more than 13
years found that engagement in leisure activities (whether as a couple or by the husband
alone) that the husband liked but not the wife, was both a cause and a consequence of the
wives' dissatisfaction. However, when couples engaged in leisure that both liked, it resulted
in the husband being happier than the wife.
2.7.4 Relationship Skills and Compatible Personalities
McNulty and Karney (2004) studied 82 couples in a four-year marriage study within
a few months of marriage. They found that couples were happier in their marriages if they
had a true view of their relationship and the skills to work through problems. Husbands and
wives with poor relationship skills and high hopes for happiness experienced deep declines
in satisfaction.
The University of Iowa's Marital Assessment Project found that shared moral values
were less important than compatible personalities for a good marriage (Klohnen, 2005).
Page 18

These married couples shared the same attitudes about faith and other values, but those with
same personalities were the happiest. Personality similarity accounted for 40 percent to 50
percent of marital satisfaction.
2.7.5 Companionship Marriage Model
In Hong Kong, it was found that there has been a shift of the traditional goal for
marriage from reproduction and survival of the family to that of attaining personal
satisfaction, mutual support from each other and

companionship (Yeung and Kwong, 1998).
Couples that had strong beliefs about the importance of marriage had a higher chance of
withstanding marital crisis. Hence, couples who have high commitment to their marriage
would not abandon their marriage when faced with a crisis (Leung et al, 2005).
2.7.6 Roles and expectations
Two studies in Singapore studied the effects of role relationships on marital
satisfaction. Lee (2001) reported in her quantitative study of 60 Chinese couples that there
was a general trend towards egalitarian role sharing in a marriage and that role conflict and
role competence were better predictors of marital satisfaction. Kwan (1992) found that the
first predictor of marital satisfaction was the relative deprivation in the marital situation,
especially for that of the wives. This was a negative relationship, i.e. the more unfavourable
a person perceives her marriage when compared with friends or relative, the lower the
marital satisfaction. The second predictor was consensus on marital role expectations and
the third best predictor was the quality of the spouse's role enactment.
Page 19

2.8 Top Ten Strengths of Happy Marriages (Enrich)
Based on a national study of 21,501 married couples from all 50 states and using a
comprehensive marital assessment tool called ENRICH which focused on 20 significant
areas and 195 questions, David Olson (2000) found that happy and unhappy couples
differed in five key areas and ranked them in order of importance: (1) how well partners

communicate, (2) how flexible they were as a couple, (3) how emotionally close they were,
(4) how compatible their personalities were and (5) how they handled conflict.
Olson also identified five other areas that affected a couple's happiness: (1) the
sexual relationship, (2) the choice of leisure activities, (3) the influence of family and
friends, (4) the ability to manage finances and (5) agreement on spiritual beliefs.
Olson's encouraged couples and professionals to focus on strengths of the marriage
rather than on only problems. He advised that, in order to build strength as a couple,
partners should pay the same sort of attention to the relationship that they did when they
were dating and to praise the other partner for the positive attributes, instead of focusing on
what bothers them about the partner.

2.9 Summary
From the literature review, there seemed to be many factors that might contribute to
marital satisfaction and happiness. However, not many relate to the relative importance of
these factors, except for Olson's Top Ten marital strengths. In my research, I have
Page 20

attempted to take factors that relate to marital satisfaction into account and incorporated
them into the questionnaire.
The Enrich Satisfaction Scale (Olson, 1996) was used to measure the dependent

variable - marital satisfaction. From the literature review, I identified and synthesized 8
major domains of marriage to explore the effects they have on marital satisfaction. The
following 8 independent variables were examined:
1. Consensus (agreement or disagreement) on 6 areas (money/ finance, religion,
handling in-laws, amount of time spend together, household chores and
children).
2. Conflict Styles (adapting from Satir's 4 stress stances).
3. Common leisure activities.
4. Confiding in spouse.
5. Commitment to marriage.
6. Sexual frequency.
7. Sexual satisfaction.
8. Communication (assessment of whether it is a problem in 5 areas in marital
relationship - talking to each other, emotional connection, feelings of taken for
granted, whether spouse knows one well, spending time together).
To find out more about how people view their marriage based on different level of
marital satisfaction, the following opinion questions were asked:
1. Whether they will marry the same person again if they were to live their lives
over again.
Page 21

2. Whether they have considered divorce before.
3. Ranking in terms of importance on what keeps a marriage going –
commitment, common goals, agreement on sexual life, open communication,
resolving conflicts and love/support.

4. Whether they seek counseling for marital issues.
5. Who they will approach if they need help.
The rest of the questionnaire asked for background of the respondent such as

cohabitation, duration of cohabitation, whether parents are divorced or not, number of years

married, whether this was their first marriage or not, gender and number of children from

current and previous marriage(s). The remaining independent variables dealt with ethnicity,

age, income level, educational level, occupation, religion. For added possible co-relations,

respondents were also asked to give information on these independent variables of their

spouse.

3

THEORETICAL FRAMEWORK

There are many theories that relate to intimate relationships, marriages and families.

However, no one theory can explain all aspects of married life. I have listed below selective

frameworks which seemed able to explain marital relationships and marital satisfaction to

some extent. However, in my approach when designing and analyzing the research, I have

adopted the strengths perspective which I find more beneficial and helpful for couples in

helping them to build happy and successful marriages.

3.1 Exchange Theory

Exchange theory is based on the principle that we enter into relationships in which

we can maximise the benefits to us and minimise our costs (Nye, 1978). We form

associations that we expect to be rewarding, and we tend to stay away from relationships

that bring us pain. At the least, we hope that the rewards from a relationship will be

proportional to the costs (Aldous, 1977).

People seek different things in relationships. For example, people marry for many

different reasons. Some of these are love and companionship, sex, procreation, status,
prestige, power and financial security. People are usually satisfied with relationships that at
least partially fulfill their expectations and that do not exceed the price they pay. In onesided relationships where one person does most of the giving and the other the receiving,
sometimes the giver becomes resentful and may seek a more equal exchange.
Page 23

Equity theory is a variation of the exchange theory that proposes that exchanges
between people have to be fair and balanced so that they mutually give and receive what is
needed. People cooperate in finding mutual fulfillment rather than compete for rewards.
They learn that they can depend on each other to meet needs and their commitment involves
strong motivations to please each other (DeGenova and Rice, 2002).
Before marriage, the Exchange Theory can explain the behavior of courting couples.
Singles seek out potential eligible partners whom they think will meet the criteria of their
soul mate. In a courting relationship, a couple gives each other priority and they invest time,
effort and money in it. There is a reciprocal relationship of give and take. When couples
think that the other partner can give them what they want (such as companionship, love,
sex, security, financial stability etc) in a marriage, they make the decision to get married.
As newly wed couples adjust to each other, they are confronted with many issues
that will need to be discussed over the course of their marriage journey. Instead of thinking

for themselves, they now need to consider the needs of their spouse. In short, if the "two can
truly become as one", they will have successfully make the "marital adjustment" which will
lead to marital stability. Exchange Theory can explain divorce in the sense that once
couples believe that they are not getting what they want from the marriage, they will call it
quits. This line of explanation may readily explain the divorce behavior of couples who are
childless at the time of divorce. However, for couples who already have children and who
have an unhappy marriage, Social Exchange Theory is not sufficient to explain why some
of them remain married, albeit unhappily.
Page 24

3.2 Life Cycle/ Family Development Theory
Beyond social exchange theory, other theories will need to come into play. We can
look at marriage at different phases – courtship, honeymoon period, arrival of children,
preschoolers, schooling children, empty nest syndrome, and retirement. Family
Development Theory states that at each of these stages, couples need to be able to grow and
develop the appropriate developmental tasks, roles, behaviors and responsibilities in order
for the marriage to function successfully (Duvall, 1977). For the family to continue to grow,
biological requirements, cultural imperatives, and personal aspirations need to be satisfied
during each stage of the family life cycle (DeGenova and Rice, 2002).
(A) Wallerstein's nine development tasks for successful marriage
Nine specific developments tasks were identified and further

elaborated by
Wallerstein (1995). She believed that couples need to successfully complete these tasks in
order that their marriage can be a successful one. These nine development tasks were:
(1) Separating from the Family of Origin
- To separate emotionally from the family of one's childhood so as to invest
fully in the marriage and, at the same time, to redefine the lines of connection
with both families of origin.
(2) Building togetherness and creating autonomy
- To build togetherness by creating the intimacy that supports it while carving
out each partner's autonomy. These issues are central throughout the marriage
but loom especially large at the outset, at midlife, and at retirement.
Page 25

(3) Becoming parents
- To embrace the daunting roles of parents and to absorb the impact of Her
Majesty the Baby's dramatic entrance. At the same time, the couple must work
to protect their own privacy.
(4) Coping with crises
- To confront and master the inevitable crises of life, maintaining the strength of
the bond in the face of adversity.
(5) Making a safe place for conflict
- To create a safe haven for the expression of differences, anger, and conflict.
(6) Exploring sexual love and intimacy
- To establish a rich and pleasurable sexual relationship and protect it from the
incursions of the workplace and family obligations.

(7) Sharing laughter and keeping interests alive
- To use laughter and humor to keep things in perspective and to avoid boredom
by sharing fun, interests, and friends.
(8) Providing emotional nurturance
- To provide nurturance and comfort to each other, satisfying each partner's
needs for dependency and offering continuing encouragement and support.
(9) Preserving a double vision
- To keep alive the early romantic, idealized images of falling in love while
facing the sober realities of the changes wrought by time.
Page 26

(B) Pat Love's 4 Stages of Love
Love (2001) identified 4 phases of love. If couples understood the processes and
dynamics of the different love stages and the roles each play, they would be better prepared
and could live a happy and satisfied married life. The first 3 stages of love - infatuation,
post-rapture and discovery are seen as leading to a deeper level of true love which she
called "connection".
3.3 Feminist Theory
Feminist theory is often called a "perspective" rather than a theory because it
reflects thinking across the feminist movement and includes a variety of viewpoints that
focus on the inequality of power between men and women in society and especially in
family life (DeGenova and Rice, 2002). The central theme is the issue of gender roles,
especially traditional gender roles. Gender is defined as the learned behaviour and
characteristics associated with being male or female, and

*feminist theories examine how
gender differences are related to power differences between men and women. Feminists
asserts that the female experiences is just as important and valuable as the male experiences
in life but that women are exploited, devalued and oppressed (Osmond and Thorne, 1993).
In general, the feminists have challenged the definition of family based on
traditional roles. They see family as a dynamic and diverse system whose members are
constantly changing, and it should not confine men or women to prescribed roles. While
they may have been socialized to perform particular roles (for example the male as provider
and decision-maker and females as passive and nurturing), feminists maintain that both men
and women can play various roles and be functional in all of them. This perspective
Page 27*

*provides couple with more flexibility, because both men and women can play roles based
on their unique skills and interests, as opposed to the roles traditionally assigned based on
gender (DeGenova and Rice, 2002). The feminist perspective is about choice and about
equally valuing the choices individuals make. Feminists do not object to the idea of women
being "traditional or a homemaker" as long it is her choice and not a role imposed on her. In
the analysis of the research data, the researcher will examine if there are any gender
difference in marital strength factors for husbands and wives.
3.4 Strengths Perspective
Historically, most approaches to social work with families have focused on*

individual pathology and problem solving or have considered problems of a family member
to be symptoms of family dysfunction (Early and GlenMaye, 2000). The Strength
Approach to social work practice is one that value families. In the strengths perspective, the
environment is prominent as both resource and target of intervention. In line with humanist
approaches to social work, the strengths approach believes that humans have the capacity
for growth and change. This "life force" (Weick, 1992), or "the human power" (Smalley,
1967), is the drive that continually transforms and heals.
Another assumption underlying the strengths approach is that people also have
knowledge that will be important in defining their situations - the problematic aspects as
well as potential and actual solutions. Acknowledging a client's resourcefulness and
perseverance in managing a difficult situation is an opportunity for a social worker to affirm
the client's capabilities.
Page 28

Furthermore, another fundamental assumption of the strengths perspective is the
idea that human beings are resilient. Resilience means that humans often survive and thrive
despite risk factors for various types of problems and dysfunction (Anthony and Cohler,
1987; Garmezy, 1993; Haggerty, Sherrod, Garmezy, and Rutter, 1994).
The strengths perspective, as Kirst-Ashman and Hull (1997) noted, assumed that
power reside in people and that we should do our best to promote power by refusing to label
clients, avoiding paternalistic treatment, and trusting clients

to make appropriate decisions.

Two popular textbooks, for example, Generalist Social Work Practice: Empowering

Approach (Miley, O'Melia and Dubois, 1998) and The Empowerment Approach to Social

Work Practice (Lee, 1994) incorporate the principle of strengths into every phase of the

helping process. The Solutions Focused Approach also maximized client empowerment by

inviting them to take control of their lives by formulating their own goals and marshalling

their inner strengths, family and community resources (De Jong and Berg, 2002).

Within the social work practice literature, a focus on the strengths of clients has

received increasing attention in recent years. For couples who stay together, they have

found ways to remain resilient despite difficulties and challenges in their marriages. From

the strengths perspective, these couples possessed strengths and qualities that helped them

to work out their problems and to remain committed to staying in a marriage. These couples

have constructed their own solution based on their own resources and successes (De Shazer,

1988). It is the intention of this research to uncover what these strengths are and to share

this information so that couples can learn how to sustain their marriage and to enjoy

happiness and marriage longevity.

Page 29

3.5 Summary

The Singapore population is unique in the sense that even though the majority is

Chinese, the Chinese here are not the same as the Chinese in China, Hong Kong or Taiwan.

Singaporeans are a migrant society whose ancestors traditionally came from China and
India. However, through the years, its people have become cosmopolitan in their world
view and outlook. English is the main language used in business, schools as well as in most
homes. In terms of premarital and marital education, Singapore has adopted many
programmes from overseas, especially from the USA and Australia. However, many of the
values that are propagated by "western" literature are probably universal human values –
examples are communication, commitment, love and support etc. Perhaps what may be
different could be the "expression" or the actions that these values are manifested which
would be culturally influenced. However, this is not within the scope of this research.
The goal of this research is to find out what are the marital strength factors that
contribute to marital satisfaction. An attempt will also be made to see if these marital
strength factors are influenced by gender, i.e. whether these factors will be the same for
males and females. The second goal is to identify the relative importance of each of these
marital strength factors. Once we know what these marital strengths are, we can then teach
couples to do "more of what works" and for couples to learn new skills to improve their
marital satisfaction and build happy and successful marriages.

4

RESEARCH DESIGN AND METHODS

The research design for this study is a cross sectional survey which is quantitative in nature. 2 focus groups were conducted with the objective to gain an in-depth understanding of the nuances of the issues involved in a marriage relationship so as to aid me in the designing of the questionnaire. The first group comprised of 5 service providers/ professionals who worked with couples in psycho-educational workshop settings and/or individual/ couple counseling. The second group comprised of 3 married couples who were husbands and wives. However, the husbands and wives were interviewed in separate groups so as to minimize any inhibitions and the pressure to give socially desirable answers in the presence of their spouses. The summary of the focus group discussions will be presented first before discussion on the research design is presented. 4.1 Summary of findings of Focus Group Discussion with Married Couples A focus group discussion with some guide questions (See Appendix 1) was used for the focus group with married couples who have been married for more than 5 years. In fact, two couples were married for 16 years and one couple has been married for 17 years. The participants comprised of 3 married couples, i.e. a total of six persons. All the participants were university graduates and working professionals. Two couples have to travel frequently due to job demands. The wives and the husbands were interviewed separately. All participants were very aware that a marriage will change and the husband-wife relationship will mature with time. Page 31 The issues discussed include factors that are important to keep the marriage intact, the difficulties or challenges faced by these couples and how they overcome them. The focus was on the resilience and strengths of these couples. In the husband's group, there was much discussion around the issues of the need for the husbands to compromise, change and adjust to a married life from that of a bachelor's. The husbands also felt that it was important for couples to develop common interests and hobbies so that there would be common grounds to talk about. One husband said that "I feel that children are an integral part of marriage and that they (children) complete my family". However, one wife said that "we must remember that a marriage is firstly a relationship between the husband and wife and that it will be a mistake to put the children first ahead of the husband". There was consensus that a happy family was possible only if there was a happy marriage. Both husband's and wives' groups shared that it was important for couples to spend time together and to develop common hobbies or interests. They also felt that it was important to keep the romance alive and for the husbands to continue to pay attention to the wives as well as for couples to do fun things together like going for dinners and movies. The wives felt that it was important to be open in communication so that one would not be second guessing each other which would be a big pitfall for a marriage. It was interesting that the wives said that it was important not to have too high expectations (of the husbands and the marriage) but this was not mentioned in the husbands' group. Page 32 When dealing with conflicts, one wife said that "we need to focus on why you marry your husband in the first place and to remember that no one was perfect". Compromise, commitment and support for one another were identified as important ingredients in a marriage by both the husbands' and wives' groups. The importance of choice was clearly articulated by both husbands and wives - the choice to marry, the choice to work things out when things get rough and the choice to make conscious effort at building a happy marriage. 4.2 Summary of findings of Focus Group Discussion with Service Providers A similar list of guide questions was used during the focus group with service providers who worked with both premarital couples and couples. The issues discussed include the current issues faced by couples and the contents covered in premarital and marriage education. In summary, some of the challenges faced by couples involved acceptance of a spouse including things they do not like about a spouse. One professional helper suggested that it would helpful for the single person to develop a list of essentials and non-essentials characteristics of an ideal partner. The essential list would contain list of values which were more important. It was felt that there was a need to understand the person on a deeper level, and to know what both parties wanted. Many problems were not pertaining to the marriage per se, but problems that were already there, even before marriage. The group agreed that a deeper understanding of the partner was important to avoid problems in a marriage at a later time. This implied that Page 33 during the courtship period, one of the tasks was to get to know the other party on a deeper level. However, in reality, it may not be so simple, as the best part of self will be presented during courtship. Perhaps, we need to alert and encourage couples to visit and to get to know the partner's family of origin. One is often a product of our family and observing our partner spending time in their natural environment will give clues to his/ her behaviour, attitudes and values. It was raised that a common dispute item in a marriage was finance. It was felt that it was important for couples to be open in the discussion of financial issues and come to a compromise on how to manage it within a marriage. Couples must agree on their financial practices, including how much to spend and save. A service provider commented that in Singapore, there was often an unspoken tradition for a big fanciful wedding and the young

couple often got into financial debt when starting out on their marriage life together, which was not a good thing. It was felt that education played a big part and couples should be taught and persuaded to be more careful with their money. It was also observed that there appeared to be different stages of marriage. For example in the honeymoon stage, the couple will spend a lot of time together. The challenge during this period was to understand, to be open and to accept each other on a deeper level. When the children arrived, the focus will naturally be shifted to the children. If couples had not established a deeper understanding of each other, this would become a problem. It was felt that couples needed to know each other and to grow together at different stages of a marriage. They also need to accept changes to the marital relationships. Page 34 The importance of the need for personal space was highlighted, as couples needed to grow as individuals to remain interesting to each other. It was felt that couples needed to be creative in finding opportunities for time together, especially if both were working. The role of social support systems from family, friends and the community will be important in this aspect. The need to educate couples on such subjects as gender differences was also highlighted. It was felt that education plays an important role in giving the power of knowledge to couples so that they will be first of all aware of the potential pitfalls and then will be equipped with information on how to overcome these challenges. Even in parenting talk, taking care of your marriage should be highlighted. Touching on the possible contents in marriage education, there was some discussion on advocating couples to develop common hobbies so that it will promote togetherness as the couple grow old. There was some caution that we need to be mindful this might not apply to all strata of the population, for example, how do we expect the lower educated and common folks to develop interests or hobbies when they are fighting for their basic needs? In terms of the essential ingredients that make for a happy and successful marriage, the following were identified:
· Communication · Expectations (on roles, sex, money, desires)

· *Family planning Page 35* · *Family of origin (what you learn but will do differently in your family of procreation)* · *Conflict resolution, managing anger and violence* · *Individual differences (personality, values, world views, appreciation and acceptance)* · *Ask yourself if your partner will not change at all, will you still marry him/ her or love him/her as he/she was.* · *Ask yourself what behaviour and attitudes you will not accept or forgive, e.g. extra marital affairs and tell each other your bottom line. All participants felt that marriage was not a destination but a journey – a journey of personal and couple development. One must have the humility of heart to continue to learn. One must treat marriage as a deep friendship and to remember that you do not own your spouse. The creation of a successful marriage lies in your hands – you can create a loving and warm environment for each other and to be there to support and help each other. Marriage was felt to be a spiritual journey and personal development – ultimately in search of love. 4.3 Quantitative Survey The main component of the research is a quantitative survey via the use of a questionnaire (Appendix 2) that was designed based on input from the literature review and the focus group discussions. A marital instrument (Enrich Marital Satisfaction Scale) was used and incorporated as question one of the questionnaire. In the design of the responses, the Likert scale was used where appropriate. Page 36 4.4 Population and Sampling The population studied was those who were still married for 5 years and above. The original sampling design involved taking the sampling frame from the Singapore Register of Marriages as well as the Register of Muslim Marriages. However, this was not carried out due to the lack of availability of funding and the problem that the addresses on the Registry records contained the addresses of couples at the time they register for their marriage. As Singapore is a highly mobile population, the likelihood that the addresses will not be current is very high. In view of these limitations, the next best option was to use a sampling frame that has a high representation of the Singapore population. NTUC*

Income consented for the researcher to use their data base of more than 1.8 million insurance policy holders to select the sample. NTUC Income is the largest insurance company in Singapore. Globally, Singapore has one of the highest rates of ownership of computer and access to the internet. According to the Statistics Singapore Newsletter March 2006, an overall 74% of Singapore households own a computer at home. Those living in private housing had a higher percentage of computer ownership (93%) compared to those living in public housing (68%). Almost two in three households had access to internet at home (Lee, 2006). Hence, it was decided that the most efficient way for the survey to be carried out is online via the internet. The reason for choosing couples who are married for at least 5 years was because the Singapore law required that the couple be separated for at least 3 years before they can Page 37 proceed for divorce (Singapore Statues, Part X, Chap 1, 94 (1)). Hence, 5 years will eliminate any couples who have separated or are in the process of divorce proceedings during the early years of marriage. Choosing those who were married for more than 5 years also meant that couples have passed the "critical first 3 years" when most marriages break down. In the attempt for the research to be representative, the sample was selected and stratified according to the Singapore's ethnic representation. According to the Singapore Department of Statistics (2005), the ethnic composition was 76.8% Chinese, 13.9% Malay, 7.9% Indian and 1.4% others. 4.5 Sample Size and Response Rate The sample size was 3,000. The number of respondents received was 317. Eventually, 7 respondents had to be excluded as they did not fulfill the requirement of having married for a minimum of 5 years or the responses were not complete. The final number of respondents was 310 which gave a good return rate of 10.3% according to existing norms using internet surveys. After stratifying according to ethnic representation and those who were married five years or more, the survey questionnaire was sent out via the internet to respondents randomly selected from the data base of NTUC Income. Page 38 4.6 Statistical Procedures The data was analyzed using SPSS statistical programme version 14.0, to give descriptive statistics and to perform correlations, cross tabulations and multiple regression analysis. 4.7 Ethics In the letter of invitation to respondents and in the introduction to the on-line survey, respondents were informed that participation in the research was entirely voluntary and confidential. Hence, by submitting the on-line survey, respondents have implied their consent to participate in the research. 4.8 Dependent Variable The dependent variable was marital satisfaction. This was measured by the weighted Enrich Marital Satisfaction Score which I have developed as a refinement of Dr. David Olson's 10 items Enrich Marital Satisfaction Scale. This is further elaborated in Chapter 5. 4.9 Independent Variables The independent variables - "marital strength factors" were operationalised as those factors that aid in making a marriage happy. The variables included in the questionnaire were: - consensus on issues such as finances, religion, handling in-laws, time together, household chores and children - conflict styles - common leisure activities Page 39 - confiding in spouse - commitment to marriage - sexual frequency - sexual satisfaction - communication - cohabitation before marriage - duration of cohabitation - whether parents were divorced - years of marriage - other independent variables were included - such as age; ethnicity; educational level; income; occupation; religion; for both respondents and their spouses and whether first marriage, number of children etc. 4.10 Control Variables There were two control variables: a) Firstly, the subject must still be married at the time of the survey. b) Secondly, only those who were married 5 years and above were included in the research. 4.11 Highlights of Survey Questions Please refer to Appendix 2 for the full questionnaire that was used in the research. The following section highlights some of the questions and the composite scores developed in the process in order to analyse the data collected. Page 40 4.11.1 Question #1: Enrich Marital Satisfaction Scale Question 1 was Dr Olson's Enrich Marital Satisfaction Scale (see Appendix 2 and 3) which comprised of ten items and used a five point Likert scale. Respondents were asked to respond to a statement from strongly disagree, disagree, undecided, agree to strongly agree. This measured the dependent variable, i.e. marital satisfaction. The ten questions required respondents to rate how happy or unhappy they were in regard to these ten areas, which measured the affective aspect (i.e. satisfaction level) of the marital relationship. From this scale, I derived a weighted marital satisfaction score which is described in detail under Chapter 5. 4.11.2 Question # 2: Self Assessment This global question to measure respondent's self assessment of the state of their happiness in their current marriage was adapted from Locke-Wallace Marital Adjustment Test (Locke and Wallace, 1959) and Dyadic Adjustment Scale (Spanier, 1976). On a scale of 1 to 10, the respondents had to rate how happy they were with their current marriage. The self assessment score was used in the regression analysis to derive the weighted marital satisfaction score. Again, this is elaborated in Chapter 5. 4.11.3 Question # 3: Areas of Consensus Respondents were asked to indicate how frequently they agree or disagree on a 6- point Likert scale with their spouse on 6 items: Money and finance; Religion; Handling inlaws; Amount of time together; Household Chores and Children. As an independent Page 41 variable, a composite consensus score was developed which was calculated based on the mean of the 6 items. This composite score was used in multiple regression analysis. 4.11.4 Question # 4: Conflict Style Satir (1991) identified 4 stress stances – Blaming, Distraction, Rational and Leveling Stances. The first three stances were considered as "unhealthy" ways of communication and the ideal mode of communication was that of "leveling" where people could see and solve the problem rationally, including to communicate their feelings as well. Question # 4 was adapted from Satir's 4 stress stances. However, I have expanded the response for the "Blaming stance" into 2 responses, i.e. "blaming self" or "blaming spouse" in order to be more specific. The other responses; "Distract attention from the problem"; "Solve problem objectively without getting emotionally involved"; and "Communicating and working through the problem and feelings with spouse" correspond to the other 3 stances of Distraction, Rational and Leveling. 4.11.5 Question # 6: Whether Marry the Same Person Respondents were asked if they could live their life over again, would they "Marry the same person"; "Marry a different person" or "Not marry at all". The hypothesis was that respondents with high marital satisfaction will tend to marry the same person. Conversely, those with low marital satisfaction may wish that they could marry a different person or even not marry at all. Page 42 4.10.6 Question # 8: Whether considered Divorce Before This is similar to Question # 6, in the sense that respondents with high marital satisfaction would not have considered divorce. Conversely, those with low marital satisfaction may have considered divorce during the course of their marriage. 4.11.7 Question # 12: Composite Communication Score To measure the communication health of the marital relationship, respondents were asked 5 statements and to indicate whether these were a problem or not in their marital relationship. These 5 areas were "Just simply talking to each other"; "Staying emotionally in touch with each other"; "Feeling taken for granted"; "Feel that my spouse knows me well" and "Spending time together". If the answer was "A problem", a score of "1" was assigned, while "2" was assigned if the answer was "Not a problem". A cumulative score was then calculated for each respondent. Hence, the maximum score will be 10 which indicate good communication, while the minimum score will be 5. 4.11.8 Other useful questions Other questions were also included to yield more insights into Singapore's marital relationships. For example, in Question # 13, respondents were asked to rank 6 items in terms of importance to their marriage. These were commitment to the marriage; common life goals and aims; agreement on sexual life; open communication; resolving conflicts together; and finally, love and support for each other. Help seeking behaviour of couples were also asked in Question # 16 and 17. Page 43 4.12 Limitations The limitation of this research was that the 310 respondents represented about 10% of the sample of 3,000 for the on-line survey conducted. Hence, the results of the research reflected the marital relationships of these 310 respondents. We do not have the data of the 90% who did not respond to on-line survey, especially those who are happily married but did not respond. Another limitation could be the problem of respondents answering the survey in a "socially desirable" manner. On the other hand, since this was an on-line survey and there was no face-to-face encounter, there was no pressure on the part of the respondents to please the "interviewer/ researcher. On-line survey also offered the assurance of complete anonymity. Hence, respondents may in fact be encouraged to give true and honest answers. Although the sample was not random in the true sense of the word i.e. selected from all marriages in Singapore, I have highlighted earlier that this is an impossible task given that the records kept by the Registry of Marriage are of couples at the point of registration of their marriages As the records are not updated, it would be impossible to obtain current information such as addresses and contact numbers of couples to conduct a meaningful random sampling. However, efforts have been made to ensure that the sample size of 3,000 was randomly selected from NTUC huge data base of over 1.8 million policy holders, after stratifying for those who are married for 5 years and more and according to Singapore ethnic composition. The profile of the 1.8 million policy holders is similar to the ethnic composition and profile of the Singapore population in terms of income level except for perhaps the bottom 20% of the Singapore population who may be too poor to purchase an Page 44 insurance policy. Hence, one limitation of this study is that the results may not represent that of the bottom 20% population. To understand the marriages of this population, a targeted research would need to be carried out. As this was an on-line survey, those who responded to the research may be those who were IT-savy and hence, these respondents may be skewed towards those who were had higher education. However, as pointed out earlier, the households in Singapore has one of the highest rates of computer, internet ownership and IT literacy (Lee, 2006).

Singaporeans are also used to using the internet to do official transactions from filing their taxes, checking their central provident funds to registering their marriages. Furthermore, it would be difficult to obtain 310 respondents by any other methodology. Bearing these limitations in mind, using the on-line survey to reach out to respondents was still the best possible method at the point of conducting the research. Due to the nature of this research, the on-line survey was completed by only one party, i.e. either the husband or the wife. Hence, it was not possible to explore the relationship and interaction between the husband and wife in relation to marital satisfaction.

5

RESULTS AND DATA ANALYSIS

The data collected from the on-line survey was analyzed using the SPSS statistical

package version 14.0. The resulting descriptive statistics, correlations and multiple

regressions are presented below.

5.1 DEPENDENT VARIABLE: MARITAL SATISFACTION

5.1.1 Enrich Marital Satisfaction Scale (EMS)

The ENRICH Marital Satisfaction Score (EMS) developed by Dr David Olson et al

was included in the survey questionnaire as question 1 to measure marital satisfaction (See

Appendix 2). I was able to examine the reliability of this instrument.

Respondents were asked to rate how happy or unhappy they were in ten different

areas of a marriage using a five point Likert scale ranging from strongly agree, disagree,

undecided, agree and strongly agree. These ten questions are:

Q1. I am happy with how we make decisions and resolve conflict.

Q2. I am unhappy with our communication and feel my partner does not understand me.

Q3. I am happy with how we share our responsibilities in our *household.*

Q4. I am unhappy with some of my partner's personality characteristics or personal
habits.

Q5. I am happy with how we manage our leisure activities and the time we spend
together.

Q6. I am unhappy about our financial position and the way we make financial decisions.

Q7. I am pleased with how we express affection and relate sexually.

Q8. I am unhappy with the way we (will) each handle our responsibilities as parents.

Q9. I am happy with our relationship with my parents, in-laws, and my partner's friends.

Q10. I feel very good about how we each practice our religion beliefs and values.

Page 46

Table 2: Enrich Marital Satisfaction item statistics
10 items Mean Std. Deviation N
Happy about how we "make decision and
resolve conflict" 3.80968 1.039310 310
Happy about "communication" 3.51935 1.205951 310
Happy about sharing of "household
chores" 3.75484 1.134010 310
Happy about "partner's personal
characteristics/ habits" 3.07419 1.197751 310
Happy about "leisure activities and time
together" 3.74839 1.097768 310
Happy about "finance position and finance
decisions" 3.48387 1.261092 310
Happy about "expression of affection and
relating sexually" 3.59355 1.155803 310
Happy about "parental responsibilities" 3.43548 1.157793 310
Happy about "external relationships with
parents, in-laws and partner's friends" 3.74516 1.022193 310

Happy about "religious beliefs and values" 4.10645 .974575 310

The Cronbach's Alpha was a high of 0.889 for the Enrich Marital Satisfaction ten
items scale. As can be seen from the table above, the range for the items was from a
minimum of 3.074 to a maximum of 4.106. The standard deviation was not big, with a
variance of 0.076. For the ten items, the mean was 36.27 with a standard deviation of 7.95.
The result was very good when compared with Olson's national sample of 21,501
married couples which reported a mean of 32.2 and a standard deviation of 8.6. (Olson and
Olson, 2000).
The respondents in this research reported a mean score of 36.27 which represented a
high marital satisfaction score which meant that "they were satisfied with most aspects of
their couple relationship" (See interpretation of score in Appendix 3).
Page 47

5.1.2 Self Assessment Marital Satisfaction (SAS)
In the survey, I included a summary question (Question 2) which asked respondents
to rate how happy they were with their current marriage on a scale of 1 to 10; 1 being
extremely unhappy and 10 being perfectly happy. From the data analysis, it was found that
the minimum score for SAS was 1 and the maximum score was 10. The mean was 7.19 with
a standard deviation of 2.5.
The SAS allowed me to refine the EMS and developed a new methodology to

measure marital satisfaction which I called "Weighted EMS".
5.1.3 Weighted Enrich Marital Satisfaction Score (Weighted EMS)
Improving on Dr Olson's EMS' implicit assumption of equal weightings
One of the studies I conducted was to test the goodness of fit of Dr Olson's Enrich
Marital Satisfaction (EMS) Index. This instrument, derived from a score which is the sum
of ten variables, has been widely used in the field.
As stated in the preceding paragraph, Dr Olson's Enrich Marital Satisfaction Scale
(EMS) showed a high reliability in my sample with an overall Alpha value of 0.889. In an
attempt to fine tune and build on Dr Olson's method for measuring marital satisfaction, I
developed a Weighted EMS Score.
In Dr Olson's EMS, there was an implicit assumption, from simply adding the
scores of these ten items, that they were weighted equally, i.e. that they affect marital
Page 48

satisfaction equally. A question that I asked was "Is there a way to measure the
appropriateness of this central assumption of EMS"? Yes. It was done by asking
respondents a global question (Question Number 2 on the questionnaire, i.e. "On a scale of
1 to 10, please rate how happy you are with your marriage") to measure Self Assessment
Score (SAS). This was then used as the dependent variable. The EMS was the explanatory
variable. I then explored whether empirical data will suggest differently.
It was found that there were substantial differences in the importance of the

variables as determined by the t-tests, which ranged from 3.71 for satisfaction with common

leisure activities to 0.68 for agreement on financial decisions (see Table 3 below).

From an empirical perspective, it was found that conducting regressions using the

Weighted EMS produced slightly higher Adjusted R squares and t values than using

unweighted EMS as a dependent variable. Hence, in deriving the model for predicting

marital satisfaction in Chapter 6, independent variables were regressed against the Weighted

Enrich Marital Satisfaction Score (Weighted EMS).

More important than the statistics, however, was the concept. There was no reason

to suppose that each of the 10 items used in Dr. Olson's methodology would be equally

important in explaining a successful marriage. More than the adjusted R squares and t

values, this was the rationale for deriving a weighted EMS. Page 49

Table 3: EMS variables weighted by beta scores
EMS variables weighted by beta scores
Name of Variable t-test score Beta EMS weight*
Happy about how we "make
decision and resolve conflict"
3.52 0.198 0.177
Happy about "leisure activities and
time together"
3.71 0.191 0.171
Happy about "communication" 2.70 0.144 0.129
Happy about sharing of
"household chores"
2.30 0.119 0.107
Happy about "external
relationships with parents, in-laws

and partner's friends"
2.59 0.113 0.101
Happy about "partner's personal
characteristics/ habits"
2.30 0.101 0.091
Happy about "expression of
affection and relating sexually"
1.84 0.091 0.082
Happy about "parental
responsibilities"
1.64 0.073 0.065
Happy about "religious beliefs and
values"
1.36 0.057 0.051
Happy about "finance position and
finance decisions"
0.68 0.029 0.026
Total 1.116 1.000

Notes: (i) Y = SAS. X = the 10 components of EMS. (ii) Weights for each variable
were determined as a per cent of the sum of beta scores.
(iii) Adjusted R square for this regression was .626.
*(iv) * p<.05*
As can be seen from the table above, the weights of each of the ten items were
determined as a per cent of the sum of the beta scores. Only the first six items had a t-value
of more than 2. "Making decisions" (t-value of 3.52) had the highest weight of 0.177,
followed by "leisure time" (t-value of 3.71) with a weight of 0.171, "communication" (tvalue of 2.70) with a weight of 0.129, "household chores" (t-value of 2.30) with a weight of 0.107, "external relationships" (t-value of 2.59) with a weight of 0.101 and "personal
habits" (t-value of 2.30) with a weight of 0.091.
Page 50

The remaining four variables, Affection, Parental Responsibilities, Religious Beliefs
and Financial Decisions had t values of less than 2.
5.2 INDEPENDENT VARIABLES
There were a total of 317 respondents but 7 cases has to be excluded due to reasons
that either they did not meet the requirement of having been married for at least 5 years or
that the responses were not complete. Hence, in the end, the total number of valid responses
was 310.
5.2.1 Ethnic Distribution
Table 4: Ethnic distribution
Ethnicity Frequency Percent
Chinese 250 80.6
Malay 26 8.4
Indian 27 8.7
Others 7 2.3

Total 310 100.0

A total of 3,000 cases were selected from the sampling frame and were invited to
respond to the survey. In the attempt for the sample to be representative of the Singapore
population, the sample was stratified according to the national ethnic distribution (see
Section 2.3). The actual returns saw the Chinese comprising the majority of the respondents
who responded to the survey at 80.6%. The number of Malays and Indians who responded
were almost equal at 8.4% and 8.7% respectively and Others made up the rest of the
remaining 2.3%. It was found that there was no significant correlation between marital
satisfaction and ethnicity.
Page 51

5.2.2 Gender Distribution
There was almost an equal distribution of females (50.5%) and males (49.5%) who
responded to the survey.
5.2.3 Years of Marriage
Table 5: Years married
Years Married Frequency Percent
5 – 9 years 115 37.3
10 – 14 years 57 18.5
15 – 19 years 43 14.0
20 – 24 years 39 12.7
25 – 29 years 32 10.4
30 years and above 22 7.1
Total 308 100.0

The table above shows the breakdown of the duration of years of marriage of
respondents in intervals of 5 years. The majority (37.3%) of respondents were married
between 5 to 9 years. 18.5% were married for between 10 to 14 years, 14% were married
for between 15 to 19 years, 12.7% were married for between 20 to 24 years, 10.4% were
married for between 25 to 29 years and 7.1% had marriages lasting 30 years or more, with
the longest duration being 41 years of marriage. No significant correlation was found
between marital satisfaction and duration of marriage for this sample.
5.2.4 Respondent's Education
The majority of the respondents had university education (37.1%) while 22.9% had
some form of diplomas, 11.9% had polytechnic education, 12.9% had upper secondary
education, 14.5% had secondary education and only 0.6% had primary level education.
There was no significant correlation between marital satisfaction and educational level.
Page 52

The sample was similar when compared with Singapore's educational level of
working adults, with the same percent of the population who had University education
(37.1%). 15% had other diplomas, 19.8% had polytechnic education and 27.9% had upper
secondary education (Singapore Statistics Department, 2001). In this sample, there was 10%
more than the national profile who had other diplomas. There was a possibility that
respondents in this study who had upper secondary or

polytechnic education may have
taken courses to upgrade themselves and hence they reported
that they have "other
diplomas". This was not surprising as Singapore encourages
life long learning.

5.2.5 Respondent's Income
The majority of the respondents (64.7%) earned between
$1,000 and $5,000 per
month. This was made up of 34% with an income bracket of
$1,000 to $3,000 and another
30.7% earning $3,001 to $5,000. 10.5% had income less than
$1,000 or no income, while
the remaining 24.8% earned above $5,000. This was made up
of 12.7% who earned $5,001
to $7,000, 5.2% with income between $7,001 and $9,000 and
6.9% with income more than
$9,000. There was no significant correlation between marital
satisfaction and income level.
Compared with Singapore's working population, there was a
similar pattern in terms
of distribution across the income levels, in that the majority
of Singaporeans (74.3%) earned
between $1,000 and $5,000, with another 14% earning more
than $5,000. The remaining
11.7% earned less than $1,000. It was noted that there was
10% more respondents in the
study who earned above $5,000.
Page 53

5.2.6 Respondent's Occupation
The majority of the respondents were either in management
and administration jobs
(36.6%) or were professionals (24.8%). 12.7% categorized
themselves as students, followed
by 10.8% in the technical industry, 8.8% in the service
industry, 5.9% were homemakers
and 0.3% were production workers. There was no significant

correlation between marital
satisfaction and occupation.
5.2.7 Respondent's Religion
The majority of the respondents were Buddhist (34.2%). This corresponded to the
ethnicity of the respondents as 80.6% were also Chinese. The next biggest group was
Christians (29%), followed by those with no religion (18.2%), Muslims (10.4%), Hindus
(5.6%) and others (2.6%). There was no significant correlation between marital satisfaction
and religion.
5.2.8 Parents Divorced
93.4% of the respondents came from intact families whereas only 6.6% of the
respondents came from families where their parents were divorced. There was no
significant correlation between marital satisfaction and whether the respondent's parents
were divorced or not.
5.2.9 First Marriages
93.2% of the respondents reported that this was their first marriage, while only 6.8%
reported that they were divorced before. There was no significant correlation between
marital satisfaction and whether it was the respondent's first marriage or not.
Page 54

5.2.10 Number of Children of Current Marriage
Table 6: Number of children current marriage
No. of Children Frequency Valid Percent
0 61 19.7
1 64 20.6
2 118 38.1
3 53 17.1
4 14 4.5

Total 310 100.0
The above table shows the frequency distribution of the number of children the
respondents had. The mean was 1.66, the median was 2 and the mode was 2. There was no
significant correlation between marital satisfaction and number of children of the current
marriage or previous marriages.
5.2.11 Number of Children of Previous Marriages
Table 7: Number of children from previous marriage
No. of Children Frequency Percent Valid Percent
Remarriages 0 8 2.6 38.1
1 3 1.0 14.3
2 9 2.9 42.9
3 1 .3 4.8
Total 21 6.8 100.0
First marriages 289 93.2
Total 310 100.0
Out of the 310 cases, 21 were remarriages and 289 were first marriages. Of the 21
respondents who had been divorced, 38.1% had no children from their previous marriage(s).
14.3% had 1 child, 42.9% had 2 children and the remaining 4.8% had 3 children from their
previous marriage(s). There was no significant correlation between marital satisfaction and
whether there were children from previous marriages.
Page 55

5.2.12 Factors Relating to Spouse
Respondents were asked to give information relating to their spouses' age,
education, income, occupation and religion. When these were correlated with marital
satisfaction, it was found that there were no significant correlation between these
independent variables and marital satisfaction.

5.2.13 Cohabitation

The majority of the respondents (83.5%) did not cohabitate with their partners

before marriage. Only 16.5% did. It was found that was no correlation between cohabitation

and marital satisfaction.

5.2.14 Sex Frequency

Table 8: Sex frequency

Frequency per month Frequency Percent

O times 52 18.5

1 – 4 times 126 44.8

5 – 8 times 59 21.0

9 to 12 times 28 10.0

13 – 16 times 7 2.5

More than 17 times 9 3.2

Total 281 100.0

Respondents reported their sexual frequency ranging from 0 to 28 times per month.

The majority (44.8%) had sex 1 to 4 times per month, followed by 21% who had sex 5 to 8

times per month. The mean was 4.7 times per month. This finding was consistent, although

lower than the Durex survey (2005) finding of 73 times a year or 6 times a month for

Singaporeans. Singapore was ranked as the bottom second after Japan for being the least

Page 56

sexually active country with people having sex out of a total of 41 countries and 317,000

respondents (Durex Global Sex Survey, 2005).

It was noted that quite a sizeable 18.5% did not have sex at all. Hence, further

analysis was conducted on how this group scored on their self rating of their sexual

satisfaction (see Table 9 below).

Table 9: Sexual satisfaction and Sex frequency (N=52)

Satisfaction Level when
sex frequency = 0 Percent
Very dissatisfied 17.0
Dissatisfied 12.5
Neutral 29.0
Satisfied 29.0
Very satisfied 12.5
Total 100.0
Table 9 showed a surprising high percentage of respondents (41.5%) reporting that
they were either satisfied sexually (29%) or very satisfied sexually (12.5%) with their
spouse even though they were not having sex. Hence, the relationship between sexual
satisfaction and sexual frequency was not so simple and straight forward. Lee (2001) also
found in her sample that the average frequency of sexual activity for couples who were high
in marital satisfaction were lower that those who were low in marital satisfaction.
According to social exchange theory, these respondents reported that they were sexually
satisfied because they could be getting satisfaction from other areas. McCarthy (1998)
defined sex as not just sexual intercourse but advocated that couples should engage in sex
that comprised on a continuum ranging from touch, sensual touch, playful touch, erotic
Page 57

touch to intercourse. This area warrant further research to fully understand the relationship
between sexual frequency and sexual satisfaction of couples in Singapore.
5.2.15 Sexual Satisfaction
Table 10: Sexual satisfaction
Satisfaction Level Frequency Percent

Very dissatisfied 24 7.9
Dissatisfied 31 10.2
Neutral 89 29.2
Satisfied 120 39.3
Very satisfied 41 13.4
Total 305 100.0
The majority were satisfied with the frequency of sex. 52.7 percent reported that
they were either satisfied (39.3%) or very satisfied (13.4%) with their sex life. There
appeared to be a significant relationship between sex frequency and sexual satisfaction. The
adjusted R square coefficient was .325 and the t value was 12.149 for Weighted EMS,
(p<.001).
5.2.16 Communication
(A) Communication Status
Question 12 asked respondents the current status of their marriages (whether it is a
problem area or not) in the 5 areas which are represented in the following tables.
Page 58

Table 11: Five Areas of communication
5 Areas of Communication Not a
Problem
A Problem Total
Talking to each other 275
(89.3%)
33
(10.7%)
308
(100%)
Emotional connection 253
(82.1%)
55
(17.9%)

308
(100%)
Feel taken for granted 206
(67.1%)
101
(32.9%)
307
(100%)
Spouse does not know me well 208
(68.2%)
97
(31.8%)
305
(100%)
Spending time together 239
(77.3%)
70
(22.7%)
300
(100%)

As can be seen from the above tables, the majority of the respondents said that it
was not a problem in the following areas: talking to each other (89.3%); staying emotionally
in touch with each other (82.1%); feeling taken for granted (67.1%); feeling that their
spouses do not know them well (68.2%) and finally; spending time together (77.3%).

However, it was noticed that there was a higher percentage of respondents who felt
taken for granted (32.9%), that their spouse did not know them well (31.8%) and who may
not be satisfied with the amount of time spend together (22.7%). Further analysis and
correlation of these variables with marital satisfaction was conducted by developing a
composite communication score.

(B) Communication – Composite Scores

From the five sub-questions of Question 12, a composite score for communication
was developed. A score of 1 was assigned if the respondent answered "A problem" and a
score of "2" was assigned if the answer was "Not a problem". The maximum score was 10
and the minimum score was 5, with a higher score indicating better communication. The
correlation with marital satisfaction using the Weighted EMS and composite
communication score was statistically significant, with an adjusted R-square of .602 and a t-
Page 59

value of 21.485 (p<.001). Hence, this was consistent with research findings that those with
better communication will tend to have higher marital satisfaction level (DeGenova and
Rice, 2002; Olson, 2000; Gottman, 1998).
5.2.17 Consensus
Respondents were asked to rate their degree of agreement or disagreement on 6
areas – money/ finance; religion, handling in-laws; amount of time spent together,
household chores and children in Question 3. As can be seen from the table 11 below, a
total of 91% of the respondents agreed to some degree on all the five areas, with 53.9%
almost always agreeing; 11.9% always agreeing and another 25.2% occasionally agreeing
on these areas with their spouse.
Table 12: Consensus
Degree of Agreement Frequency Percent
Always disagree 2 0.6
Almost always disagree 8 2.6
Frequently disagree 18 5.8
Occasionally agree 78 25.2

Almost always agree 167 53.9
Always agree 37 11.9
Total 310 100.0
Composite Consensus Score
A composite mean conflict score was created from these 6 sub-questions. It was
found that the correlation was significant when the composite mean conflict score was
correlated with Weighted EMS. The adjusted R square was .540 and the t value was 19.063
Page 60

(p<.001). Hence, the higher the mean consensus score the higher the level of marital
satisfaction. The importance of helping couples to develop skills to deal with disagreements
cannot be over-emphasized (Curran, 1983).
5.2.18 Conflict Resolution Styles
Question 4 on identification of conflict styles used during conflicts was designed for
use in marital relationships. This was adapted from the 4 stress stances by Virginia Satir
(1991) – Blaming, Distraction, Rational and Leveling. According to Satir, the best mode is
leveling where both parties are able to solve their conflicts by communicating and working
through the problem as well as feelings with each other.
Respondents were asked to identify their conflict styles from 5 options:
1) Blame my spouse
2) Blame myself
3) Distract attention from the problem
4) Solve problem objectively without getting emotionally involved and
5) Communicate and work through the problem and feelings with my spouse.
As elaborated earlier, blaming spouse and blaming self was

collapsed into one
category. The correlation between marital satisfaction and
conflict style was significant,
with a coefficient of .251 for adjusted R square and t value of
10.163 for Weighted EMS
(p>.001). Those who adopted the Leveling mode of resolving
conflict were more satisfied
with their marriages.
Page 61

To see if there was any difference in conflict resolution styles
by gender, a crosstabulation was conducted.
(A) Conflict resolution styles by Gender
Table 13: Conflict resolution styles by Gender
Conflict Styles Gender Total
Male Female
1. Blame spouse 32
(21.1%)
17
(11.2%)
49
(16.1%)
2. Blame self 7
(4.6%)
8
(5.3%)
15
(4.9%)
3. Distract from problem 16
(10.5%)
11
(7.2%)
27
(8.9%)
4. Solve problems objectively without
getting emotionally involved
25

(16.4%)
41
(27.0%)
66
(21.7%)
5. Communicate and work through
problems and feelings together
72
(47.4%)
75
(49.3%)
147
(48.4%)
Total 152
(100%)
15 2
(100%)
304
(100%)
When confronted by a conflict situation, the majority of the respondents (48.4%)
communicated and worked through their problems and feelings together. The findings were
significant with a Pearson's value of 9.524 (p<.005).
When styles of conflicts used were analyzed to see if there were any difference in
the conflict styles used by male and female, it appeared that the majority of both male
(47.4%) and female (49.3%) used the level communication i.e. to communicate and work
through problems and feelings together. However, there was a difference in the next
preferred style used between males and females.
Page 62

More males "blame their spouse" (21.1%), followed by 16.4% trying to "solve

*problems objectively without getting emotionally involved",
with another 10.5% using the
"distraction" method and finally 4.6% ended up "blaming
themselves".*

*For the female, the second preferred conflict resolution style
was to "solve problems
objectively without getting emotionally involved" (27%),
followed by 11.72% "blaming the
spouse", 7.2% using the "distraction" method and another
5.3% "blaming themselves".*
Page 63

(B) Conflict resolution styles and Marrying decision
*Table 14: Crosstabulation: Conflict styles and whether marry
same person*
Marry same person Total
Conflict Styles Not marry
at all
Marry
different
person
Marry
same
person
1 Count 10 21 18 49
% within Conflict Style 20.4% 42.9% 36.7% 100.0%
% within marry same person
revised 23.3% 28.0% 9.6% 16.0%
2 Count 6 5 4 15
% within Conflict Style 40.0% 33.3% 26.7% 100.0%
% within marry same person
revised 14.0% 6.7% 2.1% 4.9%
3 Count 5 9 13 27
% within Conflict Style 18.5% 33.3% 48.1% 100.0%
% within marry same person

revised 11.6% 12.0% 6.9% 8.8%
4 Count 10 19 38 67
% within Conflict Style 14.9% 28.4% 56.7% 100.0%
% within marry same person
revised 23.3% 25.3% 20.2% 21.9%
5 Count 12 21 115 148
% within Conflict Style 8.1% 14.2% 77.7% 100.0%
% within marry same person
revised 27.9% 28.0% 61.2% 48.4%
Total Count 43 75 188 306
% within Conflict Style 14.1% 24.5% 61.4% 100.0%
% within marry same person
revised 100.0% 100.0% 100.0% 100.0%
Legend for Conflict Styles:
1. Blame Spouse 2. Blame Self 3. Distract from problem
4. Solve problems objectively without getting emotionally involved
5. Communicate and work through problems and feelings together
The Pearson Chi-Square was a significant 42.848 (p<.005) when conflict styles were
cross-tabulated with the decision as to whether respondents will marry the same person or
not.
Page 64

From the above table, a significantly high percentage of respondents (61.4%) who
said that they will marry the same person resolved conflicts by "communicating and
working through their problems and feelings together". Another 20.2% who said that they
will marry the same person "solve their problems objectively without getting emotionally
involved".
5.2.19 Common Leisure Activities
It was found that marital satisfaction is significantly

correlated with whether couples
have common leisure activities. The adjusted R Square coefficient was .371 for Weighted
EMS and the t value was 13.52. This was consistent with the study that couples who
engaged in common leisure activities are happier (Crawford, 2002).

5.2.20 Commitment
(A)Crosstabulation: Commitment and Whether Marry Same Person
Table 15: Commitment and Whether marry same person
Marry Decision Total
Commitment Not Marry At All Different Person Same Person
Absolutely not
committed
0
(0%)
0
(0%)
1
(100%)
1
(0.3%)
Not committed 1
(25%)
3
(75%)
0
(0%)
4
(1.3%)
Unsure 5
(20%)
17
(68%)
3
(12%)
25

(8.1%)
Committed 18
(15.9%)
43
(38.1%)
52
(46%)
113
(36.6%)
Absolutely
Committed
20
(12%)
14
(8.5%)
132
(79.5%)
166
(53.7%)
Total 44
(14.2 %)
77
(25%)
188
(60.8%)
309
(100%)

As can be seen from the table above, those with higher level of commitment will
tend to marry the same person. In fact, 79.5% who rated themselves as "absolutely
committed" to their marriage said that they will marry the same person.
Page 65

When it came to those who rated themselves as "committed", this relationship was

not so clear. Although 46% said that they will marry the same person, another 38.1% said

that they will marry a different person.

A regression was conducted on commitment (independent variable) and whether

respondents will marry the same person (dependent variable). The 3 marry decision options

(marry the same person; marry a different person and not marry at all) were collapsed into

only two responses. The first response option i.e. "Marry the same person" was coded as

"Yes - marry the same person" while response options "Marry a different person" and "not

marry at all" was recoded as "No – will not marry the same person" in order to see if there

is a distinct relationship between the independent and dependent variables. It was found

that the adjusted R square was.183.

(B) Marital Satisfaction and Commitment

When marital satisfaction (Weighted EMS) was regressed against the independent

variable "commitment", it was found that the adjusted R square was .198, and the t-value

was 8.78. Commitment may not be a direct predictive variable for marital satisfaction.

Commitment may explain marriage longevity but it may not necessary be a happy marriage.

This perhaps explained somewhat why respondents who rated themselves as being

committed to the marriage may end up wishing that they could marry another person if

given a second chance at marriage.

Page 66

(C) Commitment and Whether Considered Divorce
The following table shows the relationship between level of commitment and
whether respondents had ever considered divorce. The Adjusted R-square value was .181.
The t value was 8.320 and the beta was .429, p<.001.
Table 16: Crosstabulation: Commitment and Whether considered divorce
Commitment Total
Whether Considered
Divorce
1
Absolutely not
committed
2
Not
committed
3
Unsure
4
Committed
5
Absolutely
Committed

Count 0 4 14 25 14 57
% within
Considered
Divorce
.0% 7.0% 24.6% 43.9% 24.6% 100.0%
1
Yes

% within
Commitment .0% 100.0% 56.0% 22.1% 8.4% 18.4%

% of Total .0% 1.3% 4.5% 8.1% 4.5% 18.4%
Count 0 0 9 47 40 96
% within
Considered
Divorce
.0% .0% 9.4% 49.0% 41.7% 100.0%

2
Fleeting
Thought

% within
Commitment .0% .0% 36.0% 41.6% 24.1% 31.1%

% of Total .0% .0% 2.9% 15.2% 12.9% 31.1%
Count 1 0 2 41 112 156
% within
Considered
Divorce
.6% .0% 1.3% 26.3% 71.8% 100.0%

3
Never

% within
Commitment 100.0% .0% 8.0% 36.3% 67.5% 50.5%

% of Total .3% .0% .6% 13.3% 36.2% 50.5%
Total Count 1 4 25 113 166 309
% within
Considered
Divorce
.3% 1.3% 8.1% 36.6% 53.7% 100.0%
% within
Commitment 100.0% 100.0% 100.0% 100.0% 100.0% 100.0%
% of Total .3% 1.3% 8.1% 36.6% 53.7% 100.0%
Page 67

A total of 50.5% of the respondents never thought of divorcing their spouses, while
31.1% entertained thoughts of divorce at some point of their marriage and another 18.4%
said that they had thought about divorcing their spouse.
Of those who never entertained thoughts of divorce, they were either committed
(26.2%) or absolutely committed (72%) to their marriages.
Even those who had fleeting thoughts of divorce were mostly committed (49%) and
absolutely committed (41.7%) to their marriages. We need to ask ourselves how this could
be. If one was committed to one's marriage, surely one would never think of divorce? The
findings apparently did not indicate so. They showed that thinking thoughts of divorce at
some point of time in a marriage did not mean that the partners were not committed to the
marriage.
Within the group who had considered divorce, the

relationship between "whether
considered divorce" and "commitment" was not so clear-cut,
as there was a high percent of
respondents who said that they were committed (43.9%) and
absolutely committed (24.6%)
to their marriages.
As part of the report on "Does Divorce Make People Happy" by
Waite et al (2002),
it was found that of those who were very unhappy in their
marriage at one point of time,
two-thirds of those who stayed together were happy 5 years
later. Stanley and Markman
(1992) identified two components to commitment: personal
dedication and constraint.
Page 68

Stanley (2002) further hypothesized that male and female
viewed and developed
commitment differently.
Doherty (2003) believed that the two key ingredients for a
successful marriage
were commitment and intentionality. Doherty identified two
distinct kinds of commitment.
"Commitment-as-long-as" meant staying together, "not as
long as we both shall live, but as
long as things are working out for me" versus "commitment-
no-matter-what." He described
the latter as "the long view of marriage in which you do not
balance the ledgers every
month to see if you are getting an adequate return on your
investment. You are here to
stay." This long-term kind of commitment is essential,
according to Doherty, but can lead to
stale marriages if not accompanied by intentionality. Hence,
it is important for couples to
hang on in a marriage, persevere and work things out
because when they do, they may find

their marriage reaching perhaps, a higher dimension.

5.3 Other Behaviours

5.3.1 Help Seeking Behaviour

Respondents were asked to rank 5 categories of people whom they would

approached to seek advice about serious problems within a marriage. Friends were ranked

as number one (27.5%), followed by siblings (27.3%). It appeared that couples would only

approach religious leaders and counsellors as a last resort, with more people choosing

religious leaders (40.4%) over counselors (27.3%).

Page 69

5.3.2 Ranking of Important Factors in a Marriage

Respondents were asked to rank 6 variables in terms of importance that will keep a

marriage going. These 6 factors were (1) commitment to the marriage, (2) common life

goals and aims, (3) agreement on sexual life, (4) open communication, (5) resolving

conflicts together and (6) love and support for each other.

Table 17: Ranking of important factors in a marriage

Rank Commitment Common

Goals

Agreement on

Sexual Life

Open

Communication

Conflict

Resolution

Mutual Love &

Support

1 166

(53.7%)

50

(16.2%)

39
(12.7%)
80
(25.9%)
66
(21.3%)
128
(41.3%)
2 39
(12.6%)
71
(23.0)
35
(11.4%)
45
(14.6%)
50
(16.1%)
66
(21.3%)
3 12
(3.9%)
52
(16.8%)
50
(16.3%)
62
(20.1%)
46
(14.8%)
32
(10.3%)
4 25
(8.1%)
46
(14.9%)
45
(14.7%)

64
(20.7%)
51
(16.5%)
19
(6.1%)
5 40
(12.9%)
56
(18.1%)
44
(14.3%)
38
(12.3%)
68
(21.9%)
22
(7.1%)
6 27
(8.7%)
34
(11.0%)
94
(30.6%)
20
(6.5%)
29
(9.4%)
43
(13.9%)
Total 309
(100%)
309
(100%)
307
(100%)
309
(100%)

310
(100%)
310
(100%)
The table above showed the frequency counts of the ranking of the 6 variables. The
following Table 22 showed the summary of the frequency counts when the data was
analyzed, taking only the percentage of each of the variables that were ranked as number
one.
Table 18: Summary of ranking of important factors in a marriage
Factors Percent
Commitment 53.7
Mutual Love & Support 41.3
Open Communication 25.9
Conflict Resolution 21.3
Common Goals 16.2
Agreement on Sexual Life 12.7
Page 70

53.7% picked "Commitment" as the number one important factor toward keeping
the marriage intact, followed by "Mutual Love and Support" (41.3%) which was ranked
overall as second and "Open Communication" (25.9%) was ranked as third. Conflict
Resolution followed closely with a ranking at fourth place (21.3%). Common Goals was
ranked fifth (16.2%) and Agreement on Sexual Life came in sixth position (12.7%).
As stated earlier in Chapter 5.2.20 above, the relationship between marital
satisfaction, decision to marry the same person, thoughts of divorce and commitment were
not so clear cut. This would require further exploration and

*research. Lauer and Lauer
(1987) and Kaslow and Hammerschmidt (1992) found many long lasting marriages that
were unhappy as well. Hence, commitment translated into marriage durability did not
necessarily equal to marriage happiness.*

*Respondents in the survey ranked commitment as number one importance to
a marriage. Commitment was found to be important in a marriage as it was akin to
insurance for couples to know that their spouse will not walk out when the things get tough
(Doherty, 2003).*

6

MODEL FOR PREDICTING MARITAL SATISFACTION

A total of 11 independent variables found to be significant with marital satisfaction were included in the step-wise regression. 6.1 Predictive Marital Strength Factors and Weighted EMS Of the 11 independent variables, 5 were excluded from the step-wise regression equation as they were found not to contribute significantly to the dependent variable – weighted marital satisfaction (See Appendix 4). These 5 independent variables with low t values of less than 2 were excluded: Years of Current Marriage; Respondent's Income; Respondent Age; Sex Frequency and Commitment. The 6 independent variables that were found to be statistically significant and predicting marital satisfaction (in order of importance) were: a) Communication b) Consensus c) Conflict Styles d) Common Leisure Activities e) Sexual Satisfaction f) Confiding in Spouse The adjusted R square for the above model was .781 (p<.001). The model comprising of the above 6 variables was able to explain 78% of the variance in marital satisfaction. Page 72 The beta coefficients were .375 for Communication, .332 for Consensus, .167 for Conflict Styles, .113 for Common Leisure Activities, .100 for Sexual Satisfaction and .071 for Confiding in Spouse. These 6 variables were able to explain and predict marital satisfaction in order of importance, with Communication *being able to explain 37.5% of the variance in marital satisfaction, Consensus accounting for 33.2%, Conflict Styles accounting for 16.7%, Common Leisure Activities accounting for 11.3%, Sexual Satisfaction for 10% and Confiding in Spouse accounting for 7.1% in explaining the variance in marital satisfaction. Table 19: Predictive strength factors for successful marriages (Weighted EMS) Model Summary Model R R Square Adjusted R Square 1 .786(a) .618 .617 2 .854(b) .729 .726 3 .873(c) .763 .760 4 .881(d) .775 .772 5 .885(e) .783 .778 6 .887(f) .786 .781 a Predictors: (Constant), Communication score b Predictors: (Constant), Communication score, mean consensus score c Predictors: (Constant), Communication score, mean consensus score, conflict style d Predictors: (Constant), Communication score, mean consensus score, conflict style, leisure activities revised e Predictors: (Constant), Communication score, mean consensus score, conflict style, leisure activities revised, Sex Satisfaction f Predictors: (Constant), Communication score, mean consensus score, conflict style, leisure activities revised, Sex Satisfaction, Confide in Spouse Page 73 Table 20: Predictive strength factors for successful marriages (Weighted EMS) Coefficients (a) Unstandardised Coefficients Standardized Coefficients Model B Std. Error Beta t Sig. (Constant) 1 -.049 .182 -.268 .789 Communication Score .418 .020 .786 20.677 .000 (Constant) -.557 .162 -3.446 .001 Communication Score .278 .022 .522 12.703 .000 2 mean consensus score .378 .037 .425 10.337 .000 (Constant) -.465 .152 -3.059 .002 Communication Score .252 .021 .474 12.081 .000 mean consensus score .349 .035 .391 10.072 .000 3 conflict style .137 .022 .198 6.121 .000 (Constant) -.507 .149 -3.410 .001 Communication Score .230 .021 .432 10.849 .000 mean consensus score .307 .035 .344 8.653 .000 4 conflict style .128 .022 .186 5.851 .000 leisure activities revised .161 .042 .143 3.868 .000 (Constant) -.491 .147 -3.349 .001 Communication Score .210 .022 .395 9.587 .000 mean consensus score .299 .035 .336 8.539 .000 conflict style .120 .022 .173 5.488 .000 5 leisure activities revised .144 .041 .127 3.470 .001 Sex Satisfaction .076 .026 .103 2.928 .004 (Constant) -.568 .150 -3.780 .000*

Communication Score .199 .022 .375 8.901 .000 mean consensus score .296 .035 .332 8.488 .000 conflict style .115 .022 .167 5.313 .000 leisure activities revised .128 .042 .113 3.052 .003 6 Sex Satisfaction .074 .026 .100 2.863 .005 Confide in Spouse .077 .037 .071 2.083 .038 a Dependent Variable: Wt EMS Marital Satisfaction Page 74 6.2 MALE (Weighted EMS) In order to find out if there was any effect as a result of gender on the predictive strength factors, another stepwise regression was conducted for male respondents. The tables below showed the results when gender was taken into consideration. Of the 6 predictive marital strength factors, one factor, i.e. sexual satisfaction was found not to be significantly correlated with marital satisfaction and was excluded from the model. The remaining 5 predictive strength factors (in order of importance) were: a) Communication b) Consensus c) Common Leisure Activities d) Conflict Styles e) Confide in Spouse The adjusted R square coefficient was .773. The corresponding beta coefficients were .435, .310, .172, .110 and .106, p<.001. These 6 marital strength factors were able to explain the variance in marital satisfaction up to 77% of the time. Table 21: Predictive strength factors for successful marriages (Weighted EMS) Model Summary for Gender = Male Model (Male) R Square Adjusted R Square 1 .780(a) .609 .606 2 .857(b) .735 .731 3 .873(c) .763 .757 4 .880(d) .774 .767 5 .884(e) .782 .773 a Predictors: (Constant), Communication score b Predictors: (Constant), Communication score, mean conflict score c Predictors: (Constant), Communication score, mean conflict score, leisure activities revised d Predictors: (Constant), Communication score, mean conflict score, leisure activities revised, conflict style e Predictors: (Constant), Communication score, mean conflict score, leisure activities revised, conflict style, Confide in Spouse Page 75 Table 22: Predictive Strength Factors for Successful Marriages (Weighted EMS) Coefficients(a,b) Male Unstandardized Coefficients Standardized Coefficients Model B Std. Error Beta t Sig. (Constant) 1 -.200 .286 -.700 .485 Communication Score .441 .031 .780 14.179 .000 (Constant) -.860 .251 -3.429 .001 Communication Score .293 .032 .518 9.152 .000 2 mean *consensus score .424 .054 .441 7.791 .000 (Constant) -.962 .240 -4.015 .000 Communication Score .269 .031 .477 8.701 .000 mean consensus score .341 .056 .355 6.106 .000 3 leisure activities revised .248 .064 .204 3.881 .000 (Constant) -.886 .237 -3.743 .000 Communication Score .258 .031 .457 8.412 .000 mean consensus score .319 .055 .333 5.762 .000 4 leisure activities revised .233 .063 .191 3.699 .000 conflict style .082 .033 .114 2.470 .015 (Constant) -.977 .237 -4.122 .000 Communication Score .245 .031 .435 7.973 .000 mean consensus score .298 .056 .310 5.364 .000 leisure activities revised .209 .063 .172 3.320 .001 5 conflict style .079 .033 .110 2.419 .017 Confide in Spouse .118 .054 .106 2.172 .032 a Dependent Variable: Wt EMS Marital Satisfaction b Selecting only cases for which Gender = male For male respondents, communication, consensus, common leisure activities, conflict styles and confiding in spouse were predictive of marital satisfaction. It was surprising that "sexual satisfaction" was found not to be significant for males in this study. This area would be interesting for further research. On the other hand, "confiding in spouse" was important for males. Hence, husbands who confide in their spouse enjoy marital satisfaction. This parallel the findings of a Dutch study that found that men's and not women's marital satisfaction predicts their open Page 76 communication over time (Ann Van den Troost, 2005). Hence, satisfied husbands were likely to share personal experiences with their partners. 6.3 FEMALE (Weighted EMS) In the same manner, a stepwise regression was conducted for female respondents. It was found that for females, the 5 predictive strength factors (in order of importance) for marital satisfaction were: a) Communication b) Consensus c) Conflict Styles d) Sex Satisfaction e) Common Leisure Activities The predictive marital strengths for females are slightly different from that of males. "Confiding in spouse" did not seem to be important for females to predict marital satisfaction, unlike for the males. Females took others into their confidence and did not have to rely on their spouse solely (Gray, 1992). On the other hand, male do not habitually confide in others and sought out their spouses for confidence. This seemed to support the traditional view of gender differences in terms of support network and intimacy in that female had a wider support network than males (Barnett, 2005). Page 77 The adjusted R square was .782 and the beta coefficients were .370, .344, .224, .113, and .108 respectively for the 5 strength factors. These 5 marital strengths were able to explain the variance in marital satisfaction up to 78% of the time. Table 23: Predictive Strength Factors for Successful Marriages (Weighted EMS) Model Summary – Female Model R Gender = 0 (Selected) R Square Adjusted R Square Std. Error of the Estimate 1 .785(a) .616 .613 .515643 2 .848(b) .719 .715 .442785 3 .879(c) .773 .768 .399213 4 .885(d) .783 .776 .392003 5 .889(e) .790 .782 .387177 a Predictors: (Constant), Communication Score b Predictors: (Constant), Communication Score, mean consensus score c Predictors: (Constant), Communication Score, mean consensus score, conflict style d Predictors: (Constant), Communication Score, mean consensus score, conflict style, Sex Satisfaction e Predictors: (Constant), Communication Score, mean consensus score, conflict style, Sex Satisfaction, leisure activities revised Table 24: Predictive Strength Factors for Successful Marriages (Weighted EMS) Coefficients (a,b) Female Unstandardized Coefficients Standardized Coefficients Model B Std. Error Beta t Sig. (Constant) 1 .135 .238 .567 .572 Communication Score .391 .027 .785 14.497 .000 (Constant) -.294 .214 -1.373 .172 Communication Score .261 .030 .524 8.744 .000 2 mean consensus score .342 .050 .414 6.903 .000 (Constant) -.205 .194 -1.059 .292 Communication Score .228 .028 .458 8.290 .000 mean consensus score .319 .045 .386 7.119 .000 3 conflict style .162 .029 .248 5.561 .000 (Constant) -.252 .191 -1.319 .190 Communication Score .204 .029 .410 7.082 .000 mean consensus score .307 .044 .371 6.928 .000 4 conflict style .153 .029 .234 5.292 .000 Sex Satisfaction .096 .040 .118 2.406 .018 (Constant) -.267 .189 -1.415 .160 Communication Score .185 .030 .370 6.137 .000 mean consensus score .284 .045 .344 6.300 .000 conflict style .146 .029 .224 5.097 .000 5 Sex Satisfaction .091 .039 .113 2.309 .023 leisure activities revised*

.113 .055 .108 2.052 .042 a Dependent Variable: Wt EMS Marital Satisfaction b Selecting only cases for which Gender = female Page 78 CHAPTER 7: DISCUSSION 7.1 Predictive Strength Factors for Marital Satisfaction The focus of the research was to find out what were the marital strength factors that will help couples to stay married. The key contribution of this research was the building of a model that will contribute to marital satisfaction (see Table 25 below). Table 25: Summary Model for Predicting Marital Satisfaction for Weighted EMS Weighted EMS Adj R Sq Beta t Male Adj R Sq Beta t 1. Communication .781 .375 8.901 1. Communication .773 .435 7.973 2. Conflict .332 8.488 2. Conflict .310 5.364 3. Conflict Styles .167 5.313 3. Common Leisure .172 3.320 4. Common Leisure .113 3.052 4. Conflict Styles .110 2.419 5. Sexual Satisfaction .100 2.863 5. Confide in Spouse .106 2.172 6. Confide in Spouse .071 2.083 Female Adj R Sq Beta t 1. Communication .782 .370 6.137 2. Conflict .344 6.300 3. Conflict Styles .224 5.097 4. Sexual Satisfaction .113 2.309 5. Common Leisure .108 2.052 p<.05 This research showed that there were 6 main marital strength factors that could explain the variance in marital satisfaction up to 78% of the time. These were: (1) communication; (2) consensus; (3) conflict styles; (4) common leisure activities; (5) sexual satisfaction and (6) confiding in spouse. Marital satisfaction = (.375) Communication + (.332) Consensus + (.167) Conflict Style + (.113) Common Leisure Activities + (.100) Sexual Satisfaction/contentment + (.071) Confiding in Spouse Page 79 There were some gender differences in terms of the order of the four common marital strengths depending on whether the respondents were male or female. In addition, for males, "confiding in spouse" was important, whereas for the females, "sexual satisfaction" was important. For males, the following 5 marital strengths were able to explain up to 77% of the variance in marital satisfaction: Male marital satisfaction = (.435) communication + (.310) consensus + (.172) common leisure + (.110) conflict styles + (.106) confide in spouse For females, the following 5 marital strengths were able to explain up to 78% of the variance in marital satisfaction:

Female marital satisfaction = (.370) communication + (.344) consensus + (.224) conflict styles + (.113) sexual satisfaction /contentment + (.108) common leisure 7.2 Measurement of Marital Satisfaction using Weighted EMS As discussed in Chapter 5.1.3, the Weighted ENRICH Marital Scale (EMS) was a refinement over that of Dr Olson's ENRICH Marital Scale. This was because conceptually, it would seem that the 10 different questions in the EMS scale would have different weightage and contribution to the overall marital satisfaction score. Page 80 The following table shows the summary of the weights for each of the 10 items. Table 26: Summary of Weights for EMS Name of Variable EMS weight Happy about how we "make decision and resolve conflict" 0.177 Happy about "leisure activities and time together" 0.171 Happy about "communication" 0.129 Happy about sharing of "household chores" 0.107 Happy about "external relationships with parents, in-laws and partner's friends" 0.101 Happy about "partner's personal characteristics/ habits" 0.091 Happy about "expression of affection and relating sexually" 0.082 Happy about "parental responsibilities" 0.065 Happy about "religious beliefs and values" 0.051 Happy about "finance position and finance decisions" 0.026 Total 1.000 7.3 Gender Differences Sex satisfaction was important for the females and this came as a surprise because one would expect men to be more concerned about sexual satisfaction. However, it was important to note that sexual satisfaction may mean more than sex per se to the females. It may also mean intimacy, acts of affection and love other than physical love. In fact, McCarthy (1998) advocated that couples should engage all the "5 gears of touch" to increase intimacy and not just zoom to the 5ᵗʰ gear i.e. sexual intercourse. Page 81 Although common leisure activities were important for both genders, it was ranked as more important for males (3ʳᵈ position) than for the females (5ᵗʰ position). In fact, Crawford (2000) found that husbands were happier than wives when they engaged in leisure activities that they both liked. "Confiding in spouse" was one of the marital strengths for males which could predict marital satisfaction. This was not the case for females. It appeared that wives need to understand the importance of being a confidante to their husbands, although it appeared that wives do not have to depend on their husbands as the sole person when it came to confiding. 7.4 6 Marriage Pillars© To arrive at the content or curriculum to be included in the pre-marital and marriage enrichment materials, we need to take into account the 6 predictive marital strengths as identified by the stepwise regression model. These 6 marital strength factors (which I dubbed the 6 Marriage Pillars), can point the way towards helping couples strengthening and build happier marriages. The 6 Marriage Pillars© were (1) Communication (2) Consensus (3) Conflict Styles (4) Common Leisure (5) Sexual Satisfaction (or Sexual Contentment) and (6) Confide in Spouse. This is represented in the diagram below. Page 82 Table 27: Diagram of 6 Marriage Pillars© MARRIAGE PILLAR© # 1: Communication The importance of communication cannot be over emphasised. Gottman (1994) stressed the importance of positive couple interactions. Olson (2000) and DeGenova and Rice (2002) also pointed to contribution of good communication to marital satisfaction and happiness. In this study, "Communication" was the number one predictive marital strength factor for marital satisfaction. It is no wonder that Satir (1991) said that "Communication is to marriage what breathing is to life". In addition, we all know that communication is not limited to verbal communication. In fact, Chatman (1992) identified five languages of love and Love (2001) also advocated for couples to do things for each other that meant "I love you" in the other person's language. Communication Consensus Conflict Styles Sexual Contentment Common Leisure Confide in Spouse 6 MARRIAGE PILLARS© Marital Satisfaction & Happiness 1 2 3 4 6 5 Page 83 MARRIAGE PILLAR© # 2: Consensus This study found that the more the agreement on issues, the better the marital satisfaction. This seemed logically as the more harmony exist in the couple relationship, the happier the marriage. Literature also agreed that how couples handled conflicts was important in predicting marital satisfaction and happiness (Olson, 2000; DeGenova and Rice, 2002). MARRIAGE PILLAR© # 3: Conflict Styles The manner in which couples handled their differences also affected their marital satisfaction. It appeared that the healthier and more useful manner to handle conflict is to deal with it directly but with couples having a chance to voice their opinions as well as feelings. Satir (1991) called this style of handling conflict "Levelling". Wallerstein (1995) felt that if people could acknowledged that conflicts existed in all marriages and that it was only in dealing and muting those conflicts, that couples would be on their way toward building an enduring relationship. MARRIAGE PILLAR© # 4: Common Leisure This study found that "Common Leisure" was important in predicting marital satisfaction. The key word here is "common", i.e. leisure activities that both husband and wife enjoyed and can engaged in together. This was consistent with the research findings by Crawford et al (2002), although it showed that the husbands were the happier lot than their wives. Page 84 MARRIAGE PILLAR© # 5: Sexual Contentment (Sexual Satisfaction) Sex builds connection. Generally, sexual activity has two purposes - procreation and spousal unity (Stanley, 2002). Spousal unity means that sex builds attachments between the husband and wife. "Sexual Contentment" (or Sexual Satisfaction) was the number 5 predictor marital strength factor. However, when gender was controlled, "Sexual Satisfaction" was important for the females but not for the males. This will be an interesting area to conduct follow up research study to find out the nuances of the meaning of sex for male and female, and how the physical relationship between spouses helped to build and strengthen marriages. MARRIAGE PILLAR© # 6: Confide in Spouse It was found in this study that "Confiding in Spouse" was more important for males than for females. Perhaps in the local context, the gender difference that males do not go about sharing confidences of intimate nature outside of a marriage still existed. They instead turn to their spouse who is their confidante. Ann Van Den Troost (2005) found that satisfied husbands were more likely to share personal experiences with *their partners. Interestingly, this was not mirrored by the females. Singaporean females do not rely on their spouse in sharing of confidences. It may be a gender thing that females do generally have and used a wider network of support (Barnett, 2005). Hence, wives need to realize the importance of their role in providing support and being a confidante to their husbands. Page 85 7.5 5 Marriage Pillars© for Husbands and Wives From earlier discussion, it was noted that due to gender differences (see section 7.2 and 7.3), there were some slight differences and shifting of the positions for the 3rd, 4th and 5th Pillars of marital strengths for husbands and wives. The following two diagrams depict the differences between the genders. Table 28: Diagram of 5 Marriage Pillars© for Husbands Communication Consensus Conflict Styles Common Leisure Confide in Spouse 5 MARRIAGE PILLARS© FOR HUSBANDS Marital Satisfaction & Happiness 1 2 3 4 5 Page 86 Table 29: Diagram of 5 Marriage Pillars© for Wives It appeared that "common leisure" was more important for husbands than for wives, as it was the 3rd pillar for the former and the 5th pillar for the latter. Conflict styles were more important for wives (3rd pillar) than for husbands (4th pillar). For wives, "sexual contentment" is the 4th pillar but it was not significant for husbands. Instead, "confiding in spouse" was important for husbands only and it was the 5th pillar. Communication Consensus Conflict Styles Common Leisure 5 MARRIAGE PILLARS© FOR WIVES Marital Satisfaction & Happiness 1 2 3 5 Sexual Contentment*

7
RECOMMENDATIONS

The results of this research represent one of the first available indigenous data and
knowledge on Singapore marriages. As such, there will be implications for knowledge
development, practice and policy formulation. It is the hope of the researcher that this will
lead to more interest and efforts in research and development on the area of marriage and
relationships in Singapore.

8.1 Implications for Practice

The study highlighted the predictive marital strength factors that contribute to
marital satisfaction in Singapore – known as the Marriage Pillars©. In the design of public
education campaign and educational materials for dating, pre-marital and marriage
enrichment workshops, these 5 Marriage Pillars© will need to be taken into account and
incorporated into teaching materials and public education messages. These are the pillars
that couples will need to build in order to enjoy a happy and successful marriage.

In the teaching marriage education, it is important for practitioners to translate
information into bite size knowledge and to suggest practical

tips and behaviours that
couples could learn and practice in their marriage relationships. Practitioners will also need
to be mindful of gender differences as shown in the variation and order of importance of the
5 Marriage Pillars© for husbands and wives. The 5 Marriage Pillars© for males are
Communication, Consensus, Common Leisure, Conflict Styles and Confide in Spouse. The
5 Marriage Pillars© for females are Communication, Consensus, Conflict Styles, Sexual
Contentment and Common Leisure.
Page 88

Although the relationship between commitment and marital satisfaction was not so
clear cut, the majority of the respondents ranked it as the number one ingredient towards
keeping a marriage going. This could reflect a gap in cognitive understanding and emotional
connection. Knowing and being committed to the marriage does not necessary lead to
marital satisfaction. Hence, even though couples could be enjoying marriage longevity, it
may or may not be a happy one. Practitioners need to teach and point out to couples that if
they want a happy marriage, they would need to be intentional in their actions in order to
make their marriage a lasting and happy one.
Using the 5 Marriage Pillars© as a framework, practitioners could identify and affirm
the strengths of couples for those pillars that are already strong or existing in the marriage
and then to guide and coach them to build or strengthen other pillars that may be missing or
weak.
8.2 Implications for Policy/ Programmes

The Ministry of Community Development, Youth and Sports had done some good
ground breaking work in the promotion of strong marriages and building strong and stable
families. The challenges that face us now is how we can go one step further beyond
promoting marriages and focus on building the necessary infra-structure to help couples
build, sustain and enjoy satisfying marriages. Hopefully, when couples find marital
happiness, they will go on to enjoy longevity in a successful marriage, thereby contributing
to family and societal solidarity.
Page 89

Government and community support have an impact on individual's action. We
need to think creatively in the area of providing incentives for long marriages. For example,
one of the service providers who participated at the focus group suggested that at the
company level, the importance of long marriages could be recognised by giving employees
half a day off or time-off during the staff's wedding anniversary. Another participant
suggested that the Government could offer some "tangible monetary" incentive (even if it is
a token amount) that will go into the Central Provident Fund to "pay" for the couple's
apartment if a couple are married long enough, say, for every 5 or 10 years of marriage.
This would send a strong public message that lasting marriages are cherished by the society.
As preventive programmes, marriage education could become an integral part of the
school curriculum, from tertiary level down to even primary schools. Of course, the

educational programmes should be designed to be age appropriate. To be successful, there
need to be effective collaboration and cooperation between the Ministry of Education and
the Ministry of Community Development and Sports, with the support of community and
private organisations.
At the moment, couples attend premarital preparation courses on a voluntary basis.
At the ground level, agencies providing such courses felt that the greatest challenge is the
recruitment of participants for these courses. These agencies may be equipped to provide
these services, but they reckoned that marketing and promoting awareness of these courses
are not their forte and they do not have the financial resources to do so. They hoped that the
Ministry of Community Development and Sports could do more in this respect to help in
Page 90

the effective marketing and creating public awareness/ education. Perhaps, the newly
created Marriage Central under the National Family Council could fulfill this role.
Miracles will start to happen when all Singaporean couples preparing for their
wedding will also prepare for their marriage. As the saying goes "The wedding is one day,
but a marriage last for a lifetime". Taiwan already has legislated 4 hours of compulsory
premarital education. The challenge for Singapore is to take the first baby step to making
premarital education a must for all couples.

This is because there is much at stake in the successes and failures of our love lives

than just personal and private happiness. Whether our society survives or thrives depends on

whether our marriages are lasting and happy. Happy and successful marriages are the pillars

of strong and resilient families which in turn is the foundation of our society.

8.3 Implications for Further Research

This research looked at the strengths and resilience of couples who have remained

married and has identified what these marital strength factors are that will contribute to

marital satisfaction.

The sample of this quantitative research was taken from the large data base of

NTUC Income which has over 1.8 million people who hold insurance policies with the

company and therefore, will be somewhat representative of the general population of

Singapore. Although it gives a rich cross sectional analysis and data on the state of

marriages in Singapore, perhaps it would be useful to carry out qualitative and even

Page 91

longitudinal studies to be conducted with couples who rate themselves as being successfully

and happily married. By doing so, we will be able to have greater in-depth understanding of

the nuances and the type of issues, challenges and more importantly how the couples

overcome marital/ life challenges and remain happily married.

More specific research on the meaning of sexual satisfaction and its relationship

with sexual frequency; the meaning and relationship of

commitment and marital satisfaction

and the differences between gender in these issues also would be useful to help us

understand "what works" so that we could in turn teach other couples to practice more of

"what works". The impact of cultural effects on marital satisfaction as well as the cultural

expression of the different marital strength factors could be more fully explored especially

for a multi ethnic Singapore. On the other hand, 5 Marriage Pillars© could be considered as

"universal" factors/ values that no matter where you come from or your ethnic background,

it holds true for the human race. The cultural factors come to play perhaps in the expression

of these 5 Marriage Pillars© into behavioural actions and interactions. This would be an

interesting follow up research area.

On the flip side of happy marriages, it would be interesting to find out if these same

5 Marriage Pillars© are correlated with marriages that have failed. In addition, further

research could be carried out to see if the same weightage of the 5 Marriage Pillars© holds

true for different population, for example the younger married couples versus the older

married couples and for different ethnic groups.

8

CONCLUSION

Based primarily on the strength perspective, this study has focused on finding out "What Makes a Successful Marriage" instead of setting out to find the causes of divorce. This is because even when we know what the causes of divorce are, it will not help us to build successful marriages. On the other hand, finding out what are the "pillars" of a successful marriage, couples will be able to emulate and work towards a happy and successful marital relationship. Consistent with the Solution Focused approach, this study has shown couples, practitioners, educators and policy makers "What Makes a Successful Marriage" through the identification of the 5 Marriage Pillars©. Marriage is the most complex of human relationships. Yet, the amazing thing is that a happy marriage can be created. It is this belief that everyone can create a loving and warm environment in their marriage where couples could love and support each other that we continue to work with couples either in educational workshops or in therapy. As Schnarch (1991) says, marriage is the ultimate "people growing machine". I have identified 5 Marriage Pillars© that practitioners and educators could use in their design of courses for couples whether in premarital or marital enrichment workshops. These are the new 5 Cs for Singaporeans to covet if they want a successful, happy and satisfying marriages are: · Communication · Consensus · Conflict Styles · Common Leisure · Contentment (Sexually) for Wives /and Confide in Spouse for Husbands Page 93 I hope this study will help social workers and marriage educators design, plan and implement more effective marriage education programmes that will strengthen and build happy marriages. Indirectly, I also hope that this study will inform social work practitioners and counselors who work with couples in therapy with a deeper understanding of how marriage relationships worked, to look at the strengths of marriages and to focus on the critical areas in couple work. This study of 310 Singapore marriages have contributed to the building of 5 Marriage Pillars© which are, in a way, the secrets to maintaining and sustaining a happy and successful marriage. In order to build and strengthen marriages in Singapore, we need to address and provide various levels of intervention from remedial services to preventive and developmental services for different target groups of both couples and singles including the student population. We also need to bear in mind that there may be some gender differences and this will need to be addressed in the way we work with males and females, husbands and wives. Marriage is a journey within the bigger journey of life. Marriage is a journey that two people undertake together from the moment they say "I do". This journey may be undulating and filled with many challenges. Armed with these 5 Marriage Pillars©, couples may begin to intentionally build a happy married life instead of leaving it to chance. When our marriage is happy, it will contribute to the wellness of our family life and solidarity in society. ~ end ~